Praise fo. _ _ _ _ _

'There are some hugely funny bits, and some inspiring bits, and some nerdishly interesting bits, and some bits that read like essays in the *New Yorker*. There's lots to enjoy, particularly if you are, as I am, a Tina Fey fan girl'
Observer

'It is Fey's gift to be clever and human at once. *Bossypants* manages to be self-deprecating without being winsome ... Her chapter on career and children is rueful and profound ... Everything she has done has been on equal terms, but without ever turning her back on what it means to be a woman. How do I love Tina Fey. Let me count the ways ...'
Evening Standard

'Her anxiety about "teat Nazis" – women who judge other mothers for not breast-feeding – is brilliantly funny ... She's not Nora Ephron, no. Nor is she David Sedaris. But she's brittler, funnier, and rougher than both'
Sunday Times

'When comedy is so often viewed through a prism of masculine damage, excess and transgression, here's a fascinating and well-rounded account of someone a bit controlling, anxious but wise, being very, very funny'
Financial Times

'Loaded with personality, insights into power and the kind of humour that causes you to snort in public'
Time Australia

'At once surprisingly deep and deliberately light'
Big Issue

'This book may have changed my life. I am not being hyperbolic, I really mean it ... *Bossypants* didn't just make me laugh so loudly and often on public transport that people began to move away from me, it gave me a life lesson ... it's brilliant, fearless stuff that made me laugh and think and squirm with envy'
Scotland on Sunday

'A bespectacled comedy goddess ... *Bossypants* is a non-stop feast of gimlet-eyed wit'
Irish Sunday Independent

'Gorgeously rendered, breathlessly funny ... People will buy [*Bossypants*] in hopes that it is funny, and that it is, my friends, that it is. Amazingly, absurdly, deliriously funny. Everything you would hope for from this book – it's impossible to put down, you will laugh until you cry, you will wish it were longer, you can't wait to hand it to every friend you have – is true. Oh, the agony and the ecstasy of encountering the real deal ... Tina Fey remains, finally, inarguably and mercifully All That'
Los Angeles Times

'[A] dagger-sharp, extremely funny new book for which even the blurbs are clever ... *Bossypants* isn't a memoir. It's a spiky blend of humor, introspection, critical thinking and Nora Ephron-isms for a new generation ... Hilariously self-deprecating ... Ms. Fey deftly contrasts her show business and homebody aspects in Bossypants, very much the way her *30 Rock* character, Liz Lemon, flits between drudgery and fantasy ... Virtually nonstop zingers'
Janet Maslin, *New York Times*

'The book is hilarious ... Tina Fey is strong enough for a man but pH-balanced for a woman ... Ms. Fey's priorities in writing a memoir appear to have been flatulence jokes first and feminist consciousness-raising second. But what she manages to demonstrate, something I'm not sure I'd ever realised, is that flatulence jokes are a form of feminist consciousness-raising ... She doesn't need to make an intellectual argument that women are funny. She just is funny'
Curtis Sittenfeld, *New York Times*

'I received Tina Fey's new book, *Bossypants*, last Friday and read it straight through until 7:40 Saturday morning. I guess, as they say, I couldn't put it down. Not just a trite expression; in this case it is literally true ... *Bossypants* is not so much a memoir as it is a sort of here's-what-happened-and-why-I-think-this kind of book. It's honest and intimate, without any maudlin tales of childhood sorrow, no extraneous snark or hit-and-run tell-all gossip. It's just a great read from a mature thinker'
Janeane Garofalo

'Fey's ability not only to multitask but to do everything with excellence and ease – and to not be resented by other women, but admired and emulated – is the stuff of Gwyneth Paltrow's dreams ... In our increasingly dilated confessional culture, in which no personal experience is too personal to share, her refusal to do so feels not just refreshing but somehow noble ... Fey's larger accomplishment has been to exemplify a new brand of feminism'
New York Post

'Tina Fey is an uncommonly sensible, reflexively funny comedy goddess in eyeglasses ... It's Fey's custom-quality, handcrafted BS detector that makes *Bossypants* so irresistible ... Fey puts on the literary equivalent of a satisfying night of sketch comedy ... Excellent'
Entertainment Weekly

'Comic genius ... uproarious'
GQ

'Tina Fey is possibly the funniest writer alive today ... *Bossypants* is part autobiography, part guide to being a boss and all amazingly funny. Moreover, with laser-guided accuracy and irony, Fey tackles gender roles in her business and in her life, showing us, with a smile, how smart girls finish first ... I literally laughed out loud at least once a chapter'
Glamour

'The world's funniest woman'
Observer

Bossypants

Tina Fey

Bossypants

SPHERE

First published in Great Britain in 2011 by Sphere
This paperback edition published in 2012 by Sphere
Reprinted 2012 (seven times)

First published in the United States by Reagan Arthur Books/
Little, Brown and Company in 2011

MIX
Paper from
responsible sources
FSC
www.fsc.org   FSC® C104740

Sphere
An imprint of
Little, Brown Book Group
100 Victoria Embankment
London EC4Y 0DY

An Hachette UK Company
www.hachette.co.uk

www.littlebrown.co.uk

For Jeanne Fey:

Happy Mother's Day. I made this out of macaroni for you.

Contents

Bossypants

Introduction

Welcome Friend,

Congratulations on your purchase of this American-made genuine book. Each component of this book was selected to provide you with maximum book performance, whatever your reading needs may be.

If you are a woman and you bought this book for practical tips on how to make it in a male-dominated workplace, here they are. No pigtails, no tube tops. Cry sparingly. (Some people say "Never let them see you cry." I say, if you're so mad you could just cry, then cry. It terrifies everyone.) When choosing sexual partners, remember: Talent is not sexually transmittable. Also, don't eat diet foods in meetings.

Perhaps you're a parent and you bought this book to learn how to raise an achievement-oriented, drug-free, adult virgin. You'll find that, too. The essential ingredients, I can tell you up front, are a strong father figure, bad skin, and a child-sized colonial-lady outfit.

Maybe you bought this book because you love Sarah Palin and you want to find reasons to hate me. We've got that! I use all kinds of elitist words like "impervious" and "torpor," and I think gay people are just as good at watching their kids play hockey as straight people.

Maybe it's seventy years in the future and you found this book in a stack of junk being used to block the entrance of an abandoned Starbucks that is now a feeding station for the alien militia. If that's the case, I have some questions for *you*. Such as: "Did we really ruin the environment as much as we thought?" and "Is *Glee* still a thing?"

If you're looking for a spiritual allegory in the style of C. S. Lewis, I guess you could piece something together with Lorne Michaels as a symbol for God and my struggles with hair removal as a metaphor for virtue.

Or perhaps you just bought this book to laugh and be entertained. For you, I have included this joke: "Two peanuts were walking down the street, and one was a salted." You see, I want you to get your money's worth.

Anyone who knows me will tell you that I am all about money. I mean, just look how well my line of zodiac-inspired toe rings and homeopathic children's medications are selling on Home Shopping Network. Because I am nothing if not an amazing businesswoman, I researched what kind of content makes for bestselling books. It turns out the answer is "one-night stands," drug addictions, and recipes. Here, we are out of luck. But I *can* offer you lurid tales of anxiety and cowardice.

Why is this book called *Bossypants*? One, because the name *Two and a Half Men* was already taken. And two, because ever since I became an executive producer of *30 Rock,* people have asked me, "Is it hard for you, being the boss?" and "Is it uncomfortable for you to be the person in charge?" You know, in that same way they say, "Gosh, Mr. Trump, is it awkward for you to be the boss of all these people?" I can't answer for Mr. Trump, but in my case it is not. I've learned a lot over the past ten years about what it means to be the boss of people. In most cases being a good boss means hiring talented people and then getting out of their way. In other cases, to get the best work out of people you may have to pretend you are not their boss and let them treat someone *else* like the boss, and then that person whispers to you behind a fake wall and you tell them what to tell the first person. Contrary to what I believed as a little girl, being the boss almost never involves marching around, waving your arms, and chanting, "I am the boss! I am the boss!"

For me this book has been a simple task of retracing my steps to figure out what factors contributed to this person...

developing into this person...

who secretly prefers to be this person.

I hope you enjoy it so much that you also buy a copy for your sister-in-law.

Tina Fey
New York City, 2011

(It's so hard to believe it's 2011 already. I'm still writing "Tina Fey, grade 4, room 207" on all my checks!)

Origin Story

My brother is eight years older than I am. I was a big surprise. A *wonderful* surprise, my mom would be quick to tell you. Although having a baby at forty is a commonplace fool's errand these days, back in 1970 it was pretty unheard-of. Women around my mom's office referred to her pregnancy as "Mrs. Fey and her change-of-life baby." When I was born I was fussed over and doted on, and my brother has always looked out for me like a third parent.

The day before I started kindergarten, my parents took me to the school to meet the teacher. My mom had taken my favorite blanket and stitched my initials into it for nap time, just like she'd done for my brother eight years earlier. At the teacher conference my dad tried to give my nap time blanket to the teacher, and she just smiled and said, "Oh, we don't do that anymore." That's when I realized I had old parents. I've been worried about them ever since.

While my parents talked to the teacher, I was sent to a table to do coloring. I was introduced to a Greek boy named Alex whose mom was next in line to meet with the teacher. We colored together in silence. I was so used to being praised and encouraged that when I finished my drawing I held it up to show Alex, who immediately ripped it in half. I didn't have the language to express my feelings then, but my thoughts were something like "Oh, it's like that, motherfucker? Got it." Mrs. Fey's change-of-life baby had entered the real world.

During the spring semester of kindergarten, I was slashed in the face by a stranger in the alley behind my house. Don't worry. I'm not going to lay out the grisly details for you like a sweeps episode of *Dateline*. I only bring it up to explain why I'm not going to talk about it.

I've always been able to tell a lot about people by whether they ask me about my scar. Most people never ask, but if it comes up naturally somehow and I offer up the story, they are quite interested. Some people are just dumb: "Did a cat scratch you?" God bless. Those sweet dum-dums I never mind. Sometimes it is a fun sociology litmus test, like when my friend Ricky asked me, "Did they ever catch the black guy that did that to you?" Hmmm. It was not a black guy, Ricky, and I never said it was.

Then there's another sort of person who thinks it makes them seem brave or sensitive or wonderfully direct to ask me about it right away. They ask with quiet, feigned empathy, "How did you get your scar?" The grossest move is when they say they're only curious because "it's so beautiful." Ugh. Disgusting. They might as well walk up and say, "May I be amazing at you?" To these folks let me be clear.

I'm not interested in acting out a TV movie with you where you befriend a girl with a scar. An Oscar-y Spielberg movie where I play a mean German with a scar? Yes.

My whole life, people who ask about my scar within one week of knowing me have invariably turned out to be egomaniacs of average intelligence or less. And egomaniacs of average intelligence or less often end up in the field of TV journalism. So, you see, if I tell the whole story here, then I will be asked about it over and over by the hosts of *Access Movietown* and *Entertainment Forever* for the rest of my short-lived career.

But I will tell you this: My scar was a miniature form of celebrity. Kids knew who I was because of it. Lots of people liked to claim they were there when it happened. I was *there*. I *saw it*. Crazy Mike did it!

Adults were kind to me because of it. Aunts and family friends gave me Easter candy and oversize Hershey's Kisses long after I was too old for presents. I was made to feel special.

What should have shut me down and made me feel "less than" ended up giving me an inflated sense of self. It wasn't until years later, maybe not until I was writing this book, that I realized people weren't making a fuss over me because I was some incredible beauty or genius; they were making a fuss over me to compensate for my being slashed.

I accepted all the attention at face value and proceeded through life as if I really were extraordinary. I guess what I'm saying is, this has all been a wonderful misunderstanding. And I shall keep these Golden Globes, every last one!

Growing Up and Liking It

At ten I asked my mother if I could start shaving my legs. My dark shin fur was hard to ignore in shorts weather, especially since my best friend Maureen was a pale Irish lass who probably doesn't have any leg hair to this day. My mom said it was too soon and that I would regret it. But she must have looked at my increasingly hairy and sweaty frame and known that something was brewing.

A few months later, she gave me a box from the Modess company. It was a "my first period" kit and inside were samples of pads and panty liners and two pamphlets. One with the vaguely threatening title "Growing Up and

Liking It" and one called "How Shall I Tell My Daughter?" I'm pretty sure *she* was supposed to read that one and then talk to me about it, but she just gave me the whole box and slipped out of the room.

Dear Ginny,

    I finally got my "friend" today!! Yay!! It's about time! If I roller-skate while I'm MEN-STRU-HATING, will I die?

Dear Pam,

    Of course you can roller-skate! Don't be silly! But be careful of odor, or neighborhood dogs may try to bite your vagina. Friends forever, Ginny

Dear Tabitha,

    Sometimes I get stomach cramps on the first day of my period. My mom showed me some stretches I can do, but I also heard that drinking peach schnapps will work.

Dear Ginny,

    Schnapps will work. Act like you're putting orange juice in it, but then don't.

Dear Pam,

    I'm supposed to go to a pool party this week, but my "Aunt Blood" is still in town. Can I go?

Dear Tabitha,

    Of course you can still go! Modess makes great feminine-protection products that are so thick and puffy, you'll be super comfortable sitting on that bench near the pool telling everyone you're sick.

"Growing Up and Liking It" was a fake correspondence between three young friends. Through their spunky interchange, all my questions and fears about menstruation would be answered.

"How Shall I Tell My Daughter?"

As I nauseously perused "How Shall I Tell My Daughter?" I started to suspect that my mom had not actually read the pamphlet before handing it off to me. Here is a real quote from the actual 1981 edition:

> A book, a teacher or a friend may provide her with some of the facts about the menstrual cycle. But only you—the person who has been teaching her about life and growing up since she was an infant—can best provide the warm guidance and understanding that is vital.

Well played, Jeanne Fey, well played.

The explanatory text was followed by a lot of drawings of the human reproductive system that my brain refused to memorize. (To this day, all I know is there are between two and four openings down there and that the setup inside looks vaguely like the Texas Longhorns logo.)

I shoved the box in my closet, where it haunted me daily. There might as well have been a guy dressed like Freddy Krueger in there for the amount of anxiety it gave me. Every time I reached in the closet to grab a Sunday school dress or my colonial-lady Halloween costume that I sometimes relaxed in after school — "Modesssss," it hissed at me. "Modesssss is coming for you."

Then, it happened. In the spring of 1981 I achieved menarche while singing Neil Diamond's "Song Sung Blue" at a districtwide chorus concert. I was ten years old. I had noticed something was weird earlier in the day, but I knew from commercials that one's menstrual period was a blue liquid that you poured like laundry detergent onto maxi pads to test their absorbency. This wasn't blue, so...I ignored it for a few hours.

When we got home I pulled my mom aside to ask her if it was weird that I was bleeding in my underpants. She was very sympathetic but also a little baffled. Her eyes said, "Dummy, didn't you read 'How Shall I Tell My Daughter?'" I had read it, but nowhere in the pamphlet did anyone say that your period was NOT a blue liquid.

At that moment, two things became clear to me. I was now technically a woman, and I would never be a doctor.

When Did You First Know You Were a Woman?

When I was writing the movie *Mean Girls* — which hopefully is playing on TBS right now! — I went to a workshop taught by Rosalind Wiseman as part of my research. Rosalind wrote the nonfiction book *Queen Bees and Wannabes* that *Mean Girls* was based on, and she conducted a lot of self-esteem and bullying workshops with women and girls around the country. She did this particular exercise in a hotel ballroom in Washington, DC, with about two hundred grown women, asking them to write down the moment they first "knew they were a woman." Meaning, "When did you first feel like a grown woman and not a girl?" We wrote down our answers and shared them, first in pairs, then in larger groups. The group of women was racially and economically diverse, but the answers had a very similar theme. Almost everyone first realized they were becoming a grown woman when some dude did something nasty to them. "I was walking home from ballet and a guy in a car yelled, 'Lick me!'" "I was babysitting my younger cousins when a guy drove by and yelled, 'Nice ass.'" There were pretty much zero examples like "I first knew I was a woman when my mother and father took me out to dinner to celebrate my success on the debate team." It was mostly men yelling shit from cars. Are they a patrol sent out to let girls know they've crossed into puberty? If so, it's working.

I experienced car creepery at thirteen. I was walking home from middle school past a place called the World's Largest Aquarium—which, legally, I don't know how they could call it that, because it was obviously an average-sized aquarium. Maybe I should start referring to myself as the World's Tallest Man and see how that goes? Anyway, I was walking home alone from school and I was wearing a dress. A dude drove by and yelled, "Nice tits." Embarrassed and enraged, I screamed after him, "Suck my dick." Sure, it didn't make any sense, but at least I didn't hold in my anger.

Thankfully, blessedly, yelling "Suck my dick" is not

the moment I really associate with entering womanhood. For me, it was when I bought this kickass white denim suit at the Springfield mall.

I bought it with my own money under the advisement of my cool friend Sandee. I wore it to Senior Awards Night 1988, where it blew people's minds as I accepted the Sunday School Scholarship. That turned-up collar. The jacket that zipped all the way down the front into a nice fitted shape. The white denim that made my untanned skin look like a color. Just once I'd like to find an Oscars or Emmys dress as rad as this suit.

Suburban Girl Seeks Urban Health Care

It may have been a mistake to have my first-ever gynecology appointment in a Planned Parenthood on the north side of Chicago. I was twenty-three and honestly, there was no need. My whole setup was still factory-new. But I had never been and I had some insurance, so why not be proactive about my health like the educated young feminist I was? I slipped on my pumpkin-colored swing coat with the Sojourner Truth button on it and headed to their grim location in Rogers Park. All the windows were covered, and you had to be buzzed in through two different doors. This place was not kidding around.

I sat among the AIDS posters, proudly reading Toni Morrison's *Jazz*. Maybe later I would treat myself to sweet potato fries at the Heartland Café!

I was taken to an examining room where a big butch nurse practitioner came in and asked me if I was pregnant. "No way!" Was I sexually active? "Nope!" Had I ever been molested? "Well," I said, trying to make a joke, "Oprah says the only answers to that question are 'Yes' and 'I don't remember.'" I laughed. We were having fun. The nurse looked at me, concerned/annoyed. "*Have* you ever been molested?" "Oh. No." Then she took out a speculum the size of a milk shake machine. Even Michelle Duggar would have flinched at this thing, but I had never seen one before. "What's that device f—?" Before I could finish, the nurse inserted the milk shake machine to the hilt, and I fainted. I was awakened by a sharp smell. An assistant had been called in, I'm sure for legal reasons, and was waving smelling salts under my nose. As I "came to," the nurse said, "You have a short vagina. I think I hit you in the cervix." And then I fainted again even though no one was even touching me. I just went out like she had hit a reset button. I'm surprised I didn't wake up speaking Spanish like Buzz Lightyear. When I woke up the second time, the nurse was openly irritated with me. Did I have someone who could come and pick me up? "Nope!" "You're going to have to make another appointment. I couldn't finish the Pap smear." "WHY DIDN'T YOU FINISH IT WHILE I WAS OUT?" I yelled. Apparently it's against the law. Then she asked if I could hurry up and get out because she needed to perform an abortion on Willona from *Good Times*.

All Girls Must Be Everything

When I was thirteen I spent a weekend at the beach in Wildwood, New Jersey, with my teenage cousins Janet and Lori. In the space of thirty-six hours, they taught me everything I know about womanhood. They knew how to "lay out" in the sun wearing tanning oil instead of sunscreen. They taught me that you could make a reverse tattoo in your tan if you cut a shape out of a Band-Aid and stuck it on your leg. They taught me you could listen to *General Hospital* on the radio if you turned the FM dial way down to the bottom.

Wildwood is a huge wide beach — the distance from your towel to the water was often equal to the distance from your motel to your towel. And "back in the day" the place was packed exclusively with very, very tan Italian Americans and very, very burned Irish Americans. As a little kid, I almost always got separated from my parents and would panic trying to find them among dozens and dozens of similar umbrellas.

One afternoon a girl walked by in a bikini and my cousin Janet scoffed, "Look at the hips on her." I panicked. What about the hips? Were they too big? Too small? What were *my* hips? I didn't know hips could be a problem. I thought there was just fat or skinny.

This was how I found out that there are an infinite number of things that can be "incorrect" on a woman's body. At any given moment on planet Earth, a woman is buying a product to correct one of the following "deficiencies":

- big pores
- oily T-zone
- cankles
- fivehead
- lunch lady arms
- nipples too big
- nipples too small
- breasts too big
- breasts too small
- one breast bigger than the other
- one breast smaller than the other (How are those two different things? I don't know.)
- nasal labial folds
- "no arch in my eyebrows!"
- FUPA (a delightfully crude acronym for a protruding lower belly)
- muffin top
- spider veins

- saddlebags
- crotch biscuits (that's what I call the wobbly triangles on one's inner thighs)
- thin lashes
- bony knees
- low hairline
- calves too big
- "no calves!"
- "green undertones in my skin"
- and my personal favorite, "bad nail beds"

In hindsight, I'm pretty sure Janet meant the girl's hips were too wide. This was the late seventies, and the seventies were a small-eyed, thin-lipped blond woman's paradise. I remember watching *Three's Company* as a little brown-haired kid thinking, "Really? This is what we get? Joyce DeWitt is our brunet representative? She's got that greasy-looking bowl cut and they make her wear suntan pantyhose under her football jersey nightshirt." I may have only been seven or eight, but I knew that this sucked. The standard of beauty was set. Cheryl Tiegs, Farrah Fawcett, Christie Brinkley. Small eyes, toothy smile, boobies, no buttocks, yellow hair.

Let's talk about the hair. Why do I call it "yellow" hair and not "blond" hair? Because I'm pretty sure everybody calls my hair "brown." When I read fairy tales to my daughter I always change the word "blond" to "yellow," because I don't want her to think that blond hair is somehow better.

My daughter has a reversible doll: Sleeping Beauty on one side and Snow White on the other. I would always set it on her bed with the Snow White side out and she would toddle up to it and flip the skirt over to Sleeping Beauty. I would flip it back and say, "Snow White is so pretty." She would yell, "No!" and flip it back. I did this experiment so frequently and consistently that I should have applied for government funding. The result was always the same. When I asked her why she didn't like Snow White, she told me, "I don't like her hair." Not even three years old, she knew that yellow hair is king. And, let's admit it, yellow hair does have magic powers. You could put a blond wig on a hot-water heater and some dude would try to fuck it. Snow White is better looking. I hate to stir up trouble among the princesses, but take away the hair and Sleeping Beauty is actually a little beat.

Sure, when I was a kid, there were beautiful brunettes to be found — Linda Ronstadt, Jaclyn Smith, the little Spanish singer on *The Lawrence Welk Show* — but they were regarded as a fun, exotic alternative. Farrah was vanilla and Jaclyn Smith was chocolate. Can you remember a time when pop culture was so white that Jaclyn Smith was the chocolate?! By the eighties, we started to see some real chocolate: Halle Berry and Naomi Campbell. "Downtown" Julie Brown and Tyra Banks. But I think the first real change in women's body image came when JLo turned it butt-style. That was the first time that having a large-scale situation in the back was part of *mainstream* American beauty. Girls wanted butts now.

Men were free to admit that they had always enjoyed them. And then, what felt like *moments* later, boom — Beyoncé brought the leg meat. A back porch and thick muscular legs were now widely admired. And from that day forward, women embraced their diversity and realized that all shapes and sizes are beautiful. Ah ha ha. No. I'm totally messing with you. All Beyoncé and JLo have done is add to the laundry list of attributes women must have to qualify as beautiful. Now every girl is expected to have:

- Caucasian blue eyes
- full Spanish lips
- a classic button nose
- hairless Asian skin with a California tan
- a Jamaican dance hall ass
- long Swedish legs
- small Japanese feet
- the abs of a lesbian gym owner
- the hips of a nine-year-old boy
- the arms of Michelle Obama
- and doll tits

The person closest to actually achieving this look is Kim Kardashian, who, as we know, was made by Russian scientists to sabotage our athletes. Everyone else is struggling.

Even the Yellowhairs who were once on top can now be found squatting to a Rihanna song in a class called Gary's Glutes Camp in an attempt to reverse-engineer a butt. These are dark times. Back in my Wildwood days with

Janet, you were either blessed with a beautiful body or not. And if you were not, you could just chill out and learn a trade. Now if you're not "hot," you are expected to work on it until you are. It's like when you renovate a house and you're legally required to leave just one of the original walls standing. If you don't have a good body, you'd better starve the body you have down to a neutral shape, then bolt on some breast implants, replace your teeth, dye your skin orange, inject your lips, sew on some hair, and call yourself the Playmate of the Year.

How do we survive this? How do we teach our daughters and our gay sons that they are good enough the way they are? We have to lead by example. Instead of trying to fit an impossible ideal, I took a personal inventory of all my healthy body parts for which I am grateful:

- Straight Greek eyebrows. They start at the hairline at my temple and, left unchecked, will grow straight across my face and onto yours.
- A heart-shaped ass. Unfortunately, it's a right-side-up heart; the point is at the bottom.
- Droopy brown eyes designed to confuse predators into thinking I'm just on the verge of sleep and they should come back tomorrow to eat me.
- Permanently rounded shoulders from years of working at a computer.
- A rounded belly that is pushed out by my rounded posture no matter how many sit-ups I do. Which is mostly none.

- A small high waist.
- A wad of lower-back fat that never went away after I lost my "baby weight." One day in the next ten years, this back roll will meet up with my front pouch, forever obscuring my small high waist, and I will officially be my mother.
- Wide-set knockers that aren't so big but can be hoisted up once or twice a year for parades.
- Good strong legs with big gym teacher calves that I got from walking pigeon-toed my whole life.
- Wide German hips that look like somebody wrapped Pillsbury dough around a case of soda.
- My father's feet. Flat. Bony. Pale. I don't know how he even gets around, because his feet are in my shoes.

I would not trade any of these features for anybody else's. I wouldn't trade the small thin-lipped mouth that makes me resemble my nephew. I wouldn't even trade the acne scar on my right cheek, because that recurring zit spent more time with me in college than any boy ever did.

At the end of the day, I'm happy to have my father's feet and my mother's eyes with me at all times. If I ever go back to that beach in Wildwood, I want my daughter to be able to find me in the crowd by spotting my soda-case hips. I want her to be able to pick me out of a sea of highlighted-blond women with fake tans because I'm the one with the thick ponytail and the greenish undertones in my skin.

And if I ever meet Joyce DeWitt, I will first apologize

for having immediately punched her in the face, and then I will thank her. For while she looked like a Liza Minnelli doll that had been damaged in a fire, at least she didn't look like everybody else on TV.

Also, full disclosure, I *would* trade my feet for almost any other set of feet out there.

Delaware County Summer Showtime!

(All names in this story have been changed,
to protect the fabulous.)

Gay Wales

In 1976, a young Catholic family man named Larry Wentzler started a youth theater program in my hometown called Summer Showtime. It really is a terrific model for a community program. Young teenagers would put on daily Children's Theater shows for the community, giving preschoolers access to live theater at a very low cost for parents. The older kids would direct those Children's Theater shows and perform in Broadway-style musicals by night. In the process, all the kids would learn about music, art, carpentry, discipline, friendship, and teamwork. It's a fantastic program that continues to this day, and I can't recommend it highly enough.

Larry didn't set out to create a haven for gay teens, but you know how sometimes squirrels eat out of a bird feeder? Larry built a beautiful bird feeder, and the next thing you knew — full of squirrels.

I took a job as the night box office manager at Summer

Showtime because my eleventh-grade boyfriend said we'd have fun there. He promptly broke up with me to date a hot blond dancer girl to whom he is now married, God bless us every one. I should have known he and I weren't going to make it when for my seventeenth birthday he gave me a box of microwave popcorn and a used battery tester. You know, to test batteries before I put them in my Walkman. Like you give someone when you're in love.

Those first few nights of being freshly, brutally dumped and sitting alone in the box office were not so great. I was heartbroken and, because no one had central air back then, I had to cry myself to sleep on the floor under the air conditioner in my parents' room. But then, like Dorothy's in *The Wizard of Oz,* my world went from black-and-white to color. Because, like Dorothy in *The Wizard of Oz,* I was embraced by the gays. They loved me and praised me. I was so funny and so mean and mature for my age! And with my large brown eyes I really did look like a young ~~Judy Garland~~ Lorna Luft.

Before my evening shift, I would hang out with my new friend Tim, who ran the costume department. Tim had the highest, loudest voice you've ever heard. I could sit there for hours listening to him screech along to "And I Am Telling You I'm Not Going" while hot-gluing Joseph's Amazing Technicolor Dreamcoat together because none of us could really sew. Parents of the world, this is where you want your seventeen-year-old daughter spending her summer — snorting her DQ Blizzard out her nose from laughing so hard. The only person funnier than Tim was his meaner, louder, higher-pitched brother Tristan. One family, two impressively gay brothers.

That summer I got to know four families in which half the children were gay. In case you're interested from a sociological point of view, they were always Catholic and there were always four kids, two of whom were gay. What Wales is to crooners, my hometown may be to homosexuals — meaning there seems to be a disproportionate number of them and they are the best in the world!

Tristan would egg me on to trash-talk the little blondie who had "stolen" my boyfriend. Of course I know now that no one can "steal" boyfriends against their will, not even Angelina Jolie itself. But I was filled with a poisonous, pointless teenage jealousy, which, when combined with gay cattiness, can be intoxicating. Like mean meth. And guess who played Joseph in *Joseph and the Amazing Technicolor Dreamcoat,* by the way? You guessed it, old Battery-Tester Joe. I got to watch him in the show every night and then count my stubs in a four-foot room while he and the blonde left to get pizza. He would've never given her a crappy battery tester. And if he had, she probably would have shoved it up her twat and tried to turn it on. (This is the kind of mean stuff Tristan and I bonded over. Clearly it's very toxic.)

The unstated thing that Tim and I had in common was that we had crushes on all the same boys. The only difference was, I was allowed to talk endlessly about my feelings and Tim was in the half closet. Nobody thought he was straight, but he wasn't "out" either. He certainly never made a move on anyone. His crushes would manifest themselves in other ways. Tim had a real job working at Macy's, and sometimes he would use his disposable income to, you know, buy Rick McMenamin a baseball glove. "You were saying the other night after rehearsal how you needed a new glove, so...anyhoo," he'd trail off. The nice thing was, the straight boys didn't freak out about this, and they definitely kept all the free stuff.

Lots of teenage girls have taken comfort under the wings of half-closeted gay boys, but how many of us can brag that her two best friends in high school were twenty-five-year-old lesbians? I met Karen and Sharon one day in the middle of our giant thousand-seat auditorium. The kid who ran the lighting booth, a roughneck girl named Rita who would only answer to "Reet," was climbing from ladder to ladder hanging lights for *The Jungle Book* and cursing like a sailor with a corneal paper cut. Karen was the improv teacher and Sharon was the head scenic painter, and the three of us found ourselves spellbound by the spinning mobile of profanity that was hanging from the ceiling. It was like looking in the monkey cage but you can understand the monkey, and what the monkey is saying is "Fuck all these fucking zoo people." We started laughing and were inseparable for the next six years.

Karen and Sharon had been a couple at some unspecified time in the past but were now just friends with asymmetrical haircuts. We spent days and weeks doing nothing, calling one another ten times a day to schedule our nothing-doing. An entire evening could consist of renting a movie, such as *The Stepfather* or that one where spiders come out of Martin Sheen's face, and making nachos. Do you remember what a cultural phenomenon homemade nachos were? If you are under thirty, you probably don't even realize there was a time when people didn't have nachos. We just stood around eating crackers.

You know that game Celebrity that you and your friends invented in college? Well, first of all, you didn't invent it. It was developed by NASA to keep girls virgins well into their twenties. And second of all, we played it better than you because we played it four nights a week. We wore it out. "Okay, this is Joan Collins's character from *Dynasty*." "Alexis!" "No, her *full* name." "Alexis Carrington Colby Dexter!"

When we finally got tired of playing, around midnight, we would switch to a version called Celebrity Boff, in which you could only write down the names of celebrities you would sleep with. Playing Celebrity Boff with two half-closeted gay guys, two lesbians, and one straight girl made for an easy game. Jodie Foster's name was always in there four times. Antonio Banderas appealed to all sectors. "This is that same one we keep getting—" "Princess Stephanie of Monaco!"

It is a testament to my parents that they never reacted negatively to the four-year-long pride parade that marched through their house. They welcomed these weirdos (they were weirdos in other ways, not because of their sexual preference) with open arms and fed them all until they were sick. Only once did my mother say, "That Karen is a little butch, don't you think?" I feigned ignorance badly, "I not know what you mean!" and slipped out for a night of same-sex nachos and name yelling.

I guess I should also state that Karen and Sharon never hit on me in the slightest and it was never weird between any of us. Gay people don't actually try to convert people. That's Jehovah's Witnesses you're thinking of.

No one was ever turned gay by being at Summer Showtime, because that's not possible. If you could turn gay from being around gay people, wouldn't Kathy Griffin be Rosie O'Donnell by now? The straight boys quickly learned to be accepting and easygoing, and the straight girls learned *over the course of several years* to stop falling in love with gay boys.

By August, I was coming out of my gloom. I took a free afternoon dance class where we basically just did jazz runs back and forth across the lobby. The teacher called me "Frankenstein Arms" because I would move my right arm in unison with my right leg, like a Frankenstein. Since I had been thrown over for a dancer, this stung. But I persevered.

I was the youngest person in our group of friends and I always had a curfew. I was notorious for freaking out when it was time to go. It didn't matter if we were at local eatery the Critic's Choice enjoying mozzarella sticks after a rehearsal or at Tim and Tristan's house watching *Sleepaway Camp*—the one where the demonic little girl turns out to have a penis—when I had to go, I would shut a party down. "Hurry up. I don't want to get in trouble." Pleated eighties Bossypants.

When the summer was over, I had made about twenty-five new friends and was no longer weeping into my mom's radiator cover. But most of the kids in Summer Showtime went to the Catholic schools down the road or were well into their twenties, so I didn't see them as much once school started.

After the Greatest Summer

I had to take eleventh-grade health in twelfth grade. I had postponed it the year before so I could take choir and Encore Singers — it was kind of a big deal to be in both, whatever. I was alto 1, but sometimes they had me sing second soprano. I had a solo in "O Holy Night" in a performance at the mall. In downtown Philadelphia. Enough! Stop asking about it!

The health teacher, Mr. Garth, had a thick blond mustache — the universal sign of intelligence — and a rural-Pennsylvania accent that made him say "dawn" instead of "down" and "yuman" instead of "human." One day, in what I hope was a departure from the state curriculum, Mr. Garth devoted an entire period to teaching us "how to spot and avoid homosexuals." I could not believe what I was hearing.

I don't know what happened to this guy at the Teachers College of Anthraciteville, but he had some *opinions*. "These homosexuals, they'll trick ya. They'll fine out what kinda music ya like, what kinda candy ya like, then they'll invite you dawn to their house." As I listened, incredulous, I couldn't help but picture a young Mr. Garth being lured into a van by Paul Lynde. "Hey there, sonny, my friends and I were just going into the woods to enjoy some Jethro Tull and a Mars bar. Interested?" Oh, the shame that must have washed over Mr. Garth as "Minstrel in the Gallery" came to an end and he realized that was no Mars bar! But there was no turning back. He had already eaten half of it.

My blood started to boil as he continued. "If you're talking to someone and you think they might be a homosexual, just run. Just get out of there and tell the nearest adult." I stayed after class to tell him that I thought he had misspoken. "I think what you meant to say was 'child molesters,' not 'homosexuals.'" He just watched my hands move as I talked, not unlike a dog. It became clear that my school life and my Showtime life were separate.

The Greatest New Year's Eve Party of All Time

The line between Showtime friends and school friends was breached on New Year's Eve 1987.

My Summer Showtime friend Brendan had a New Year's Eve party. Brendan was a very dramatic boy who would say things to me like "Did you ever think that maybe the man that did that to your face did it to *mark* you so he could find you later in life?" See what I mean about the question being a reflection of the asker? When Brendan lost himself in a long dramatic rant, you could always shut him up by saying, "I like that monologue. Is it from *'night, Mother*?"

He had a beautiful face with pouty lips and that swoopy hair that was so popular during the second Reagan administration. He was the scenic artist under Sharon and he would do things like paint the entire floor of the stage an hour before a performance (ruining the white shorts the kids had been asked to bring in from home to be in the chorus of "Free to Be...You and Me"). Then he'd disappear for two days, emerging with a ten-page letter of apology. He was a mess, and his New Year's party was expected to be awesome.

I was a teetotaler at the time, and none of my close friends were big drinkers. I went with Karen and Sharon, and the place was already packed when we got there. The kitchen and dining room were full of Brendan's athletic Catholic school friends; the living room was packed with theater nerds. Brendan's mom had locked herself in her room upstairs. There was an unclaimed dog turd in the hall outside the bathroom.

People sat in small groups, talking about the other small groups that were just out of earshot. My ex and the dancer made a brief appearance, but I held my head high. I was wearing my best Gap turtleneck and my dates were two adult lesbians, so yeah, I was pretty cool.

The Summer Showtime kids had to weave nervously through the jocks to get to the Doritos. Brendan's long-suffering Catholic school "girlfriend," Patty, tried to bridge the gap between the two groups. A sweet, quiet girl with short curly hair and a face as Irish as a scone, Patty seemed to be the only person at the party who didn't realize what

Brendan's deal was—even the family dog had registered his disapproval again on the kitchen floor.

Brendan and I ran into each other on the front lawn. He seemed to be in a particularly Oscar Wilde mood. "May I kiss you?" he asked. Sure, who cares. After a tender, playacted non-French kiss, Brendan suddenly "came out" to me. In my experience, the hardest thing about having someone "come out" to you is the "pretending to be surprised" part. You want him to feel like what he's telling you is Big. It's like, if somebody tells you they're pregnant, you don't say, "I did notice you've been eating like a hog lately." Your gay friend has obviously made a big decision to say the words out loud. You don't want him to realize that everybody's known this since he was ten and he wanted to be Bert Lahr for Halloween. Not the Cowardly Lion, but *Bert Lahr.* "Oh, my gosh, no waaaay?" You stall, trying to think of something more substantial to say. "Is everyone, like, freaking out? What a . . . wow."

Brendan had clearly decided to make this party his debut, and he wandered through the crowd, performing his one-man show in various locations.

Bored, I tried making out with Victor Anthony, a straight kid who was cute but kind of a wang. He was the Cream of Wheat of making out. I would try it every now and then, thinking maybe I'd like it, but every time: no. He really was a stunningly bad kisser. It was as if he took a running start at your mouth. Brendan's stage kiss was way more skilled.

I went back inside and parked it with Karen and Sharon

in the theater living room, where Brendan was deep into Act II of "coming out." The Monsignor Bonner football team was peering in from the dining area, hearing all of this. "Here's a toast to being free of other people's expectations," Brendan monologued, "and loving whomever you choose." In the background, scone-face Patty was quietly giving people coasters. Jesus, she was really not getting it.

This evening was actually turning out to be quite boring. But then it happened.

One of the drunk girls from the Archbishop Prendergast side of the party wandered into the Showtime room and started making out with Alexis Catalano. Everyone froze. Patty looked on, scone-faced. This was unprecedented. Brendan talked a good game, but these two were going at it—in public! This was years before every pop singer in the world started fake lezzing out at the VMAs. It simply was not done. What would happen next? Karen and Sharon went into protective adult mode and pulled the two *wasted* girls apart and took them upstairs to a more private location.

Just then Brendan's mom—who was totally unaware of the proceedings—started screaming and throwing everyone's coats down the stairs, which shall henceforth be known as An Irish Goodnight.

Brendan's mom may have perfected my "party shutdown" move, but it didn't stop me from working it at the amateur level. I followed the four women upstairs, ducking the flying parkas, because it was almost two A.M.: my special expanded New Year's Eve curfew. Karen was my ride and we needed to get a move on. Alexis and jock girl were so drunk they could barely function. Karen and Sharon tried to convince them it was time to call it a night. They would give them a ride home. "Noooo, I loooooove herrrr," jock girl sobbed as Karen helped her get her coat on. I said I'd be waiting in the car and they needed to *hurry up*.

Meanwhile, Brendan stormed out of the house and drove away, furious—probably because he had "lost the room" when two girls started going to town on each other.

After I'd been waiting in the car twenty minutes and missed my curfew, I couldn't control my temper anymore. "Get the dykes in the car!" I screamed down Childs Avenue, banging my shoe on Karen's dashboard and leaving a slight crack. My husband could tell you that I still get this wound up when I'm trying to leave the house on a Saturday morning and nobody in my family has their shoes on. It's not a great quality.

(And just in case you were wondering, yes—when he returned later that night, Brendan tried to run Patty and his mother over with the car. I believe it earned him a Regional Theater Tony nomination.)

The Second Summer

My second year at Summer Showtime, I was promoted to be one of the Children's Theater directors. I directed shows with a cast of sixty twelve-year-olds and, I'll toot my own horn, I made some interesting directing choices. Such as pushing the Little Mermaid around on a rolling office chair papier-mâchéd to look like a large shell. Her hair only got caught in the wheels twice.

I knew everyone. I was fully immersed. "Immersed," Brendan would say. "You're so smart. Why don't I know more people who use words like 'immersed'?" And then he'd disappear for two days. He may have been a drunk.

Sharon's brother Sean was our "visiting director" for the Mainstage musical. Everyone referred to him as Equity Actor Sean Kenny. He was a member of the stage actors union! He was living the dream in a basement-level studio apartment in Hell's Kitchen with a rat problem. We were all in awe.

Sean was and is a skilled and confident director. I was excited to be his assistant director on a murder mystery musical called *Something's Afoot*.

My first job as assistant director was to make sure he didn't cast the talented blond dancer who had so easily stolen my boyfriend the summer before. I accomplished this with the persistent and skilled manipulation of a grade A bitch. I made articulate arguments as to why the other blond girl would be better. The Dancer Girl was "too overused." It would be more exciting to "use someone unexpected," and the other girl's "look" was "more British." A fat load of nonsense, but it worked. Dancer Girl was relegated to playing the title role in a Children's Theater show called *Guess Again*. Yes, her character and the show were both called *Guess Again*. A harsh punishment.

Obviously, as an adult I realize this girl-on-girl sabotage is the third worst kind of female behavior, right behind saying "like" all the time and leaving your baby in a dumpster. I'm proud to say I would never sabotage a fellow female like that now. Not even if Christina Applegate and I were both up for the same part as Vince Vaughn's mother in a big-budget comedy called *Beer Guys*.

Sean and I were Mentor and Mentee that summer. I was eighteen, he was twenty-seven. Sean taught me a lot about professional dignity. For example, this was when "call waiting" was new, and if you left Sean on the other line for more than ten seconds, he would hang up. And our show was a hit! On both nights! The cast party was in a backyard with paper lanterns. The cast and crew mingled. It was very glamorous.

Summer Showtime alum Richard D'Attelis was there. My friend Vanessa had gone to her eighth-grade dance with Richard D'Attelis, and he had picked her up wearing a baseball shirt customized with an iron-on photo of Olivia Newton-John. It said "Olivia Newton-John" in puffy letters on the front and "Totally Hot!" on the back. Richard had been the first of the Showtime boys to quietly come out after his stint at the Pennsylvania Governor's School for the Arts, an exclusive state-run arts intensive that might as well have been called the Pennsylvania Governor's Blow Job Academy. Imagine a bunch of seventeen-year-old theater boys away from home for the first time for six weeks. They were living in empty college dorms, for the love of Mike! Literally! Think of the joy and freedom they must have felt, like being on an all-gay space station. (I'm sure there were one or two straight boys there, too, and I imagine they did incredibly well with the one or two straight girls.)

Sean was flirting with Richard. We were seated at a picnic table at the party, and I realized they were playing footsie under the table. I could not contain my judgment. "What are you doing?" I demanded, trying to be funny and controlling at the same time. They ignored me. Richard got up to get a soda. I turned to Sean. "He's so cheesy and gross!" My power-of-suggestion technique had worked so well when I was screwing over that blond girl. I used any ammunition I could muster. "He smokes, you know." As the night wore on, I didn't get the hint. I stayed at the table with two people who were clearly going to hook up. I tried some sarcastic eye contact as Richard told Sean about his dream to turn *Xanadu* into a stage play. Like that would ever work.

In my mind, I was doing Sean a favor by trying to stop him from hooking up with someone regrettable. "Oh, my God. You know he's only, like, *twenty*." Sabotage *and* saying "like." I was really in a bad place.

Sean shot me a look. I was out of bounds. It's one thing to be a wisecracking precocious teen hanging out with twenty-seven year olds. It's another thing to get in the way of a grown man trying to get laid.

I don't know what happened between Richard and Sean that night, but the next day Sharon called me to say that Sean was very annoyed with the way I'd behaved. She said she had talked him down because "they all realized" that I had a crush on Sean. "It's natural." They *all* realized? They were all talking about what a baby I was and how I must have a crush on Sean? "I don't." I wept from sheer embarrassment. "I really don't." But the more I protested, the guiltier I seemed. And here, after twenty years, is the truth. I really didn't have a crush on Sean. I had reacted that way because I viscerally felt that what they were about to do was icky. The stomachache I felt had nothing to do with a crush. I had to face the fact that I had been using my gay friends as props. They were always supposed to be funny and entertain me and praise me and listen to my problems, and their life was supposed to be a secret that no one wanted to hear about. I wanted them to stay in the "half closet."

Equity Actor Sean Kenny did not live in the half closet. He had moved away to New York and was just back for a visit. He was a grown man. My reaction to his hooking up with Richard D'Attelis made me feel like Coach Garth. I stroked my thick blond mustache and thunk about what I had dawn.

It was a major and deeply embarrassing teenage revelation. It must be how straight teenage boys feel when they realize those boobs they like have heads attached to them.

I thought I knew everything after that first summer. "Being gay is not a choice. Gay people were made that way by God," I'd lectured Mr. Garth proudly. But it took me another whole year to figure out the second part: "Gay people were made that way by God, *but not solely for my entertainment*." We can't expect our gay friends to always be single, celibate, and arriving early with the nacho fixin's. And we really need to let these people get married, already.

Before the final performance of every summer, all the

kids were invited onstage and together we sang "Fill the World with Love" from *Goodbye, Mr. Chips.* Everyone would cry their heads off. It felt like the end of camp, and I imagine some of those kids had more to dread about going back to school than just boredom and health class.

With his dream of a theater program for young people, Larry Wentzler had inadvertently done an amazing thing for all these squirrels. They had a place where they belonged, and, even if it was because he didn't want to deal with their being different, he didn't treat them any differently. Which I think is a pretty successful implementation of Christianity.

We should strive to make our society more like Summer Showtime: Mostly a meritocracy, despite some vicious backstabbing. Everyone gets a spot in the chorus. Bring white shorts from home.

That's Don Fey

Let's review the cost-free techniques that we've learned so far for raising an achievement-oriented, obedient, drug-free, virgin adult: Calamity, Praise, Local Theater, and flat feet.

Another key element is "Strong Father Figure/Fear Thereof."

My dad looks like Clint Eastwood. His half-Scottish, half-German face in repose is handsome but terrifying. I searched the audience for him during the sixth-grade chorus concert and, seeing his stern expression, was convinced that he had seen me messing up the words to the *Happy Days* theme and that I was in big trouble. I spent the rest of the concert suppressing terror burps, only to be given a big hug and a kiss afterward. It took me years to realize, Oh, that's just his face.

It's my face, too, it turns out. The cheekbones later discovered there by a team of gay excavators are courtesy of my dad.

Don Fey dresses well. He has an artist's eye for mixing colors and prints. He wears tweedy jackets over sweater vests in the winter and seersucker suits in the summer. His garnet college ring shows off his well-groomed hands. He can still rock a hat.

My dad looks like he's "somebody." One day when I was visiting him on his lunch hour he ran into a couple of old high school buddies in downtown Philadelphia. "Hey, Don Fey!" one of the guys called from across the street. "Oh my God, Don Fey," the other guy said excitedly. The two African American secretaries waiting at the light with my dad whispered knowingly to each other, "That's *Don Fey.*"

Before I was born, my mother took my brother to Greece for the whole summer to visit family. When they were finally coming back, my dad washed and waxed his Chevy convertible, put on his best sharkskin suit, and drove all the way from Philadelphia to New York Inter-

national Airport to pick them up. (In those days, international travel meant dressing up, smoking on planes, wearing Pan Am slippers, and flying into New York.)

Their flight was due to arrive early in the morning, so Don Fey, who is never late for anything, got to the airport just before dawn. As he popped on his sweet lid and walked across the deserted parking lot toward the terminal, he saw two black gentlemen approaching from far away. He played it cool to hide his apprehension. He was in New York, after all, one of the world's most dangerous cities if you're from any other city, and from far away in the dark he couldn't tell if the guys were airport employees or loiterers.

As they got closer, he noticed they were staring him down. He continued to play it cool. Don Fey had grown up in West Philly, where he lived comfortably as a Caucasian minority. Of course these guys couldn't know that. His heart was beating a little faster as they came within ten feet of each other.

The guys looked at him intently, then one turned to the other and said, "That is one boss, bold, bladed motherfucker."

That's Don Fey. He's just a badass. He was a code breaker in Korea. He was a fireman in Philadelphia. He's a skilled watercolorist. He's written two mystery novels. He taught himself Greek so well that when he went to buy tickets to the Acropolis once, the docent told him, "Για τους Έλληνεςη, είσοδος είναι δωρέαν." (It's free for Greek citizens.)

Neighborhood kids would gather on our porch just to listen to him swear at the Phillies game. (Andy Musser talked too goddamn much. Games were often "over" by the sixth inning. "This goddamn game is over. The sons of bitches choked.")

When watching the Flyers, he would change the channel during commercials and he always knew *exactly* when to turn it back to catch the start of play. When my cousin marveled at this ability, my dad was matter-of-fact: "You just wait ninety seconds." Isn't everyone's brain a Swiss watch?

Don Fey is a Goldwater Republican, which is his only option. If you're Don Fey, you can't look at Joe Biden and be like, yes, I want to be led by this gentleman with the capped teeth. You're not going to listen to John Kerry pretending to empathize with you about the rising cost of your medications. You certainly aren't interested in the "unresolved father issues" that rendered Bill Clinton unable to keep his fly closed. Don Fey is not going to put up with that. Don Fey is a grown-ass man! Black people find him stylish!

Don Fey has what I would describe as pre–Norman Lear racial attitudes. Once the Bunker family met the Jeffersons, every interaction between blacks and whites was somehow supposed to be a life-changing lesson, especially for the white people. My generation carries that with us, only to be constantly disappointed by Kanye West and Taylor Swift.

The twin house I grew up in was across the street from the border of West Philadelphia where Don Fey grew up. Don Fey certainly had friends of other races and religions. He has told me a couple times about the night he kissed Lionel Hampton. He was at a jazz concert as a teenager with an all-white audience. At one point in the show, Lionel Hampton would invite a woman from the audience to dance with him, but the white girls were all too scared to be seen dancing with a black man. To ease the tension, Don Fey jumped up and fast-danced with Mr. Hampton, at the end of which Lionel Hampton kissed him on the forehead to a round of applause.

Conversely, he would tell us things like "If you see two black kids riding around on one bike, put your bike in the garage." This wasn't racism; it was experience. Those kids *were* coming from West Philly to steal bikes. The social factors that caused their behavior were irrelevant to a Depression baby. When you grow up getting an orange for Christmas, you're going to make sure the twenty-five-dollar bike you bought your kid doesn't get ripped off.

Norman Lear might want us to take time to understand that those kids went to poorly funded schools and that their parents, while loving and dignified, were unable to supervise their children's behavior because they were both at work doing minimum-wage jobs, but by then our bikes would be gone.

The late seventies were a dark time of "family meetings" about "tightening our belts." The embarrassment of Watergate led right to the Iran hostage crisis. Three Mile Island was in our state. It was always "Day 27" of something in Beirut. There was an infestation of gypsy moths killing the trees in our neighborhood.

I can definitely remember a period of time when the gas crisis, the Carter administration, and "Alan Alda's bleeding-heart liberal propaganda" were starting to wear on Don Fey's day-to-day dignity.

One Saturday my dad got it in his head that he was going to rent a rug shampooer at Pathmark and shampoo our carpets. He expressed this desire to my mother, who said nonchalantly, "Ugh, those things never work." We still had a half-empty bottle of rug shampoo from the one other time he'd tried it. But Don Fey could not be deterred, and I, his faithful servant, went with him. We rented the shampooer, bought a new full bottle of soap, and loaded them into the back of the Catalina.

When we got home I was sent to play outside so my dad could shampoo the whole first floor. I barely had my *Star Wars* figures lined up in the patch of dirt by the basement steps also known as Tatooine when I heard a commotion inside. My dad was cursing. Objects were being rumbled around. I got an instant bellyache.

The screen door flew open. The two bottles of rug shampoo were slammed onto the back porch. The rug shampooer came tumbling out the back door in a tangled mess.

"Your mother...is a witch!" my dad blurted as he came outside. He meant it literally. "She cursed me!" It would seem that the rented rug shampooer did not work. "The goddamn thing is defective."

"Defective" was a big word in our house. Many things were labeled "defective" only to miraculously turn functional once the directions had been read more thoroughly. If I had to name the two words I most associate with my dad between 1970 and 1990, they would be "defective" and "inexcusable." Leaving your baseball glove in a neighbor's car? Inexcusable. Not knowing that "a lot" was two words? Inexcusable. The seltzer machine that we were going to use to make homemade soda? Defective. The misspelled sign at the Beach Boys Fourth of July concert that read "From Sea to Shinning Sea"? Inexcusable. Richie Ashburn not being in the baseball hall of fame yet? Bullshit. (Don Fey had a large rubber stamp that said "bullshit," which was and is awesome.)

Was it too much to expect the rest of the world to care about grammar or pay attention to details? Shouldn't someone at the Pathmark have to make sure that the goddamn rug shampooers are in working order?

He carried the defective shampooer down the back steps, the hose flopping around on purpose just to annoy him. There was sudsy water inside it, sloshing around, mocking his dream of an orderly house. "Son of a bitch!" As he backed our giant car up the fifty-degree incline of our driveway, scraping the bumper, he barked, "Get the bottle of soap. Come on." I was going along for the ride back to Pathmark? Great. I looked at the two identical bottles of rug detergent on the back porch. One was new and returnable. One was six months old and half empty. But which was which? I couldn't tell! They were opaque. I knew that word because I was in the Gifted Program, but it didn't help me in that split second. *Why didn't I pick them both up to see which one was heavier? Why didn't I just bring both of them?* I would never be placed in the Common Sense Program. My dad honked the horn for me to hurry up. I grabbed a bottle and dashed for the car.

We rode in tense silence to the Pathmark. And, by the way, I get it now. I'm a working parent and I understand that sometimes you want to have a very productive Saturday to feel that you are in control of your life, which of course you are not. Children and Jimmy Carter ruin all your best-laid plans. And then your wife casts some sort of evil spell?! Inexcusable.

I followed my dad as he stormed into the Pathmark to

explain to them what kind of a country America was supposed to be. He took the bottle from me to put it on the customer service counter, and his face went red at the weight of it. I had grabbed the half-empty one.

And here was the indignity of the 1979 economy — we couldn't afford to waste the three dollars. Sure, once the Internet boom came in the nineties we'd all be throwing out half-full mouthwash because we wanted to try the new cinnamint flavor. We'd buy chamomile tea at Starbucks and not finish it. But not Don Fey. Not in 1979. He was going to have to drive home again and get that other bottle to return it. "Wait here," he said in a strangled voice.

He left me at the end of the No Frills aisle. I stood there, fighting back tears, pretty sure that it was illegal to leave your nine year old at Pathmark. Unfortunately, I was wearing a red polo shirt and shorts. With my short haircut and doughy frame, no fewer than three old ladies mistook me for a stock boy. "Young man, where are the plums?"

I only hope that one day I can frighten my daughter this much. Right now, she's not scared of my husband or me at all. I think it's a problem. I was a freshman home from college the first time my dad said, "You're going out at ten P.M.? I don't think so," and I just laughed and said, "It's fine." I feel like my daughter will be doing that to me by age six.

How can I give her what Don Fey gave me? The gift of anxiety. The fear of getting in trouble. The knowledge that while you are loved, you are not above the law. The Worldwide Parental Anxiety System is failing if this many of us have made sex tapes.

When I was a kid there was a TV interstitial during Saturday morning cartoons with a song that went like this: "The most important person in the whole wide world is you, and you hardly even know you. / You're the most important person!" Is this not the absolute worst thing you could instill in a child? They're the *most important person? In the world?* That's what they already think. You need to teach them the opposite. They need to be a little afraid of what will happen if they lose the top of their Grizzly Adams thermos.

Don Fey is from the Silent Generation. They are different from their children. They cannot be "marketed to." They don't feel "loyalty" to Barnes and Noble over Borders. If you told Don Fey that you never go to Burger King, only McDonald's, because you "grew up with the Hamburglar," he would look at you like you were a moron.

When my face was slashed, my dad held me on his lap in the car to the hospital, applying direct pressure with the swift calm of a veteran and an ex-fireman. I looked up and asked him, "Am I going to die?" "Don't speak," he said. So, yeah, he's not the kind of guy who wants to watch people eat bugs on *Survivor.* It's so clear to me how those two things are related.

My dad has visited me at work over the years, and I've noticed that powerful men react to him in a weird way. They "stand down." The first time Lorne Michaels met my dad, he said afterward, "Your father is ... impressive." They meet Don Fey and it rearranges something in their brain about me. Alec Baldwin took a long look at him and gave him a firm handshake. "This is your dad, huh?" What are they realizing? I wonder. That they'd better never mess with me, or Don Fey will yell at them? That I have high expectations for the men in my life because I have a strong father figure?

Only Colin Quinn was direct about it. "Your father doesn't fucking play games. You would never come home with a shamrock tattoo in that house."

That's Don Fey.

Climbing Old Rag Mountain

Let me start off by saying that at the University of Virginia in 1990, I was Mexican. I looked Mexican, that is, next to my fifteen thousand blond and blue-eyed classmates, most of whom owned horses, or at least resembled them.

I had grown up as the "whitest" girl in a very Greek neighborhood, but in the eyes of my new classmates, I was Frida Kahlo in leggings.

For many people, college is a time of sexual experimentation and discovery, and I am no exception. After a series of failed experiments with Caucasian men, I discovered that what I am *really* into is Caucasian men.

And I mean *Caucasian*. Maybe it's my way of rejecting my Hellenic upbringing, but I like 'em fair-skinned with old-timey manners and some knowledge of fishing. If I'm honest with myself, I can admit that I've known this ever since I saw Larry Wilcox ride a motorcycle — on the back of a flatbed camera truck — down the Pacific Coast Highway. I like white boys.

This worked out perfectly for me in college, because what nineteen-year-old Virginia boy doesn't want a wide-hipped, sarcastic Greek girl with short hair that's permed on top? What's that you say? None of them want that? You are correct. So I spent four years attempting to charm the uninterested. (It was probably good practice for my future career on a low-rated TV show.) I couldn't figure out how to play it. I couldn't compete with the sorority girls with their long blond ponytails and hoop earrings. I tried to find the white-boy-looking-to-rebel, but I wasn't ethnic enough to be an exciting departure. I wasn't Korean or African American or actually Mexican. I was just not all-the-way-white.

I realized my predicament early in my First Year. We don't say "freshman" or "senior," etc., at UVA because Mr. Jefferson felt that education is a lifelong process. Thomas Jefferson—another gorgeous white boy who would not have been interested in me. This was my problem in a nutshell. To get some play in Charlottesville, you had to be either a Martha Jefferson or a Sally Hemings.

During my First Year, I had a crush on a brainy, raven-haired boy from my dorm. This played out like the typical sexy coed letter to *Penthouse*. He would ask me at least once a day if I had ever seen the movie *Full Metal Jacket*. I would remind him that I had not. He would then describe parts of it to me. After several weeks of mistaking this for flirtation, I tried to kiss him one night by the Monroe Hill dorms and he literally ran away. Not figuratively. Literally.

I did go to one fraternity formal with a devastatingly

handsome guy named Awbrey Madison Cartwright III from Georgia. I mean, this guy looked like Clark Kent, no joke. He held my chair for me and opened doors. He was genteel and attentive. There was only one problem. Here's how our exchange went when he invited me to the formal:

> Tina sits on the steps in front of the theater building, chatting with friends from acting class. Awbrey Cartwright approaches.
>
> TINA: Hey, Awbrey, you're gay, right?
>
> AWBREY: (thrown) What? No. I was coming over here to ask if you want to go to my formal with me.
>
> TINA: Oh. Sure.

I was right, by the way. He was for dudes.

So you can see why, when I occasionally had a little success with a heterosexual white male, I dug in and hung on for dear life. And this is why I climbed Old Rag Mountain at night.

There was a kid, older than me, an architecture student who did plays in the drama department on the side. I won't use his real name because I think he'd find out about it and it would give him too much satisfaction. I'll refer to him instead by how he looked at the time, which was like a handsome Robert Wuhl. Go spend an hour trying to picture exactly what that could be and pick up the book again when you've got it.

Welcome back.

Handsome Robert Wuhl and I were in a few plays and

some acting classes together. He seemed to appreciate my sense of humor. Like all boys at that time, he tried to talk like David Letterman, which I appreciated. I don't remember how we first came to be making out in a car, but it was awesome so I kept doing it. Should it have been a "red flag" to me that these incidents would only take place under cover of night, in the back driveway behind my on-campus housing? Absolutely. Was it "not great" that there was never any actual "date" before these events and that it was a secret? Of course. But I finally had my hands on a thin-lipped white boy so everybody just shut up about it!

Secret make-out time went on for a while. Handsome Robert Wuhl claimed to have some ethical/religious reasons for not going all the way, which was fine by me, as I would have been terrified. I say "claimed" because I think it was closer to the truth that he was just a control freak who thought he should save himself for someone hot.

Sometimes there would be a big drama department event, like a party to celebrate the opening of *The Robber Bridegroom* or a wine and cheese reception to welcome guest artist Aaron Sorkin (totally true). Handsome Robert Wuhl would take a pretty date to the party while I attended with friends, and then he'd pick me up later for car sports. Sometimes we would just drive around. We hit a deer once. Why were we just driving around the Blue Ridge Mountains? To this day I do not understand what this boy was up to. Was it a control experiment to see how much boring nothingness I would put up with before we finally made out? Possibly.

We did eventually go on kind of a date. He took me to the mall to help him shop for a present for another girl, and he bought me a sandwich at Hickory Farms. "You can really eat a lot," he laughed when I finished it. I was certain that he would eventually be so impressed with my ability to eat like one of the guys that he would want me to be his girlfriend.

So when HRW asked me casually if I'd like to climb Old Rag Mountain with him, I said yes immediately, then raced home to tell my roommates. Clearly I was very special to him. Why else would he invite me to climb a nearby mountain? They were skeptical.

I met HRW the next evening at his off-campus apartment. Yes, the climb was going to be at night. I didn't question this because I didn't know anything about rock climbing and I assumed that we were in this for the romance. He introduced me to one of his roommates, Jess or Chris or something. He was a wiry little guy who would be joining us on the climb. This was news to both me and Jess-Chriss. To say he was unfriendly would be the biggest understatement since the captain of the Hindenberg said "I smell gas."* He alternated between ignoring me and shooting me disdainful looks that clearly said "Who is this ugly off-brand non-sorority girl ruining our homo-erotic bro-times?"

We drove out of town a little ways, listening to Peter

---

* Or it would be the biggest understatement since Warren Buffett said, "I can pay for dinner tonight." Or it would be the biggest understatement since Charlie Sheen said, "I'm gonna have fun this weekend." So, you have options.

Gabriel's "In Your Eyes." HRW played that song constantly. He was very deep. Did I mention yet that he always wore a small shell necklace and he told me that he was never going to take it off until Apartheid ended?

It was dusk when we got to the bottom of Old Rag, and when HRW and Jess-Chriss realized that neither of them had brought flashlights. After a quick debate about whose fault it was, they decided it didn't matter and we should just start climbing.

The first leg of our journey was the walk from the parking lot to the beginning of the actual trail. It was about a mile and a half. By the time we got to the foot of the mountain, I was already nauseous from overexertion and trying to hide it. I asked for some water.

"Aw, are you kidding me?" The two bros looked blankly at each other. They had also forgotten to bring any water.

The next, more difficult portion of the trail was the "rock scramble," a feat requiring serious concentration to find a foothold and safely navigate up, over, and in between slippery rocks. It was getting dark now, but there was bright moonlight. It was difficult, but I was actually enjoying the challenge. Jess-Chriss continued to wish I was dead and/or better looking. HRW climbed ahead of us both, showing off. I learned that night that there are markers on these kinds of trails, one color for the easy path, one color for the intermediate path. I also learned that sometimes, especially at night, these markers are hard to see.

Soon HRW told us he was "going off the trail" and he'd meet us after a while. Neither Jess-Chriss nor I was happy about this, but I guess HRW was just too good a climber to be held back. Jess-Chriss and I climbed along in silence for about twenty minutes. If Jess-Chriss had trouble finding the next marker he certainly didn't get any help from me, because I was a hiking novice. I was wearing wrestling shoes, for example. Jess-Chriss kept calling ahead to HRW to "stop showing off" and "stop being a dick." HRW would call back through the dark that he just wanted to try something and he'd be back on the trail in a few minutes. And then we heard it. A grunt and the sound of little rocks rolling down bigger rocks and then a sound like a bag of laundry bouncing and scraping down your basement steps. That idiot had fallen off the mountain.

Jess-Chriss and I must have had the same thought: "Am I going to have to explain to this kid's mother how he died?"

TINA: We were climbing Old Rag Mountain in the dark on a weeknight.

MOTHER WUHL: Is this your girlfriend, young man?

JESS-CHRISS: No.

MOTHER WUHL: Were you my son's girlfriend?

TINA: No, ma'am, but he did once tell me that I could be really pretty if I lost weight.

MOTHER WUHL: What the hell were you kids doing up there?!

TINA: Well, I can't speak for Jess-Chriss, but I was hoping for a leisurely night-climb followed by some over-the-jeans action.

JESS-CHRISS: Me, too. But then *she* was there.

We called frantically to HRW. After a few minutes, he answered. We followed his voice back down the trail and found him. Jess-Chriss climbed out onto the rocks to help HRW over to the trail. He was banged up, but it was somehow decided that we should continue up the mountain. The last half mile or so was not as steep, and we finally made it to the smooth granite top, where we sat down to take in the beautiful dark panorama of the Shenandoah Valley. HRW motioned for me to sit near him, and Chriss-Jess knew instinctively to go sit far away. Tired, dehydrated, and nauseous, I was still ready to try to make this work if there was any funny business to be had. But HRW didn't touch me. Instead he stared wistfully out at the night sky and told me about the last time he'd climbed Old Rag. It was two days prior, during daylight. He had brought his friend Gretchen up here for lunch. He really liked her, he confided in me. Liked her so much that he didn't quite know what to do about it. After they had gotten all the way to the top and had the picnic lunch he'd prepared, he offered her a piece of Trident gum, and Gretchen—he had to stop and smile at the adorableness of this—Gretchen had asked him to tear the piece of Trident in half because it was too big for her. "Can you believe that?" he marveled. A girl so feminine and perfect that half a piece of Trident was the most she could handle.

I tried to process what this meant for my evening.

"So . . . you and I will not be dry humping, then?"

*   *   *

The way down from Old Rag is a forest road. We found a stream in the woods and finally got a drink of water. We scooped it up with our hands and it was the greatest, most satisfying drink of water I ever had in my life. "Oh the water, / Get it myself from the mountain stream," I sang over and over again in my head. I was listening to a lot of Van Morrison at the time, because I was also very deep.

It was sunrise by the time HRW dropped me off. As weird as the night's events had been, I couldn't help but be excited about the fact that I had climbed a mountain. I never would have thought I could do that. I think someone should design exercise machines that reward people with sex at the end of their workouts, because people will perform superhuman feats for even the faint hope of that.

As I crawled into my bottom bunk, I thought about how I had climbed Old Rag. I thought about Gretchen, the girl who could only accommodate half a piece of gum. "I hope you marry her," I imagined saying to HRW, "and I hope she turns out to have a cavernous vagina."

Young Men's
Christian Association

At 5:10 A.M., the el train from the Morse stop in Chicago to the Davis St. stop in Evanston is surprisingly safe for young white women. The only people on the train at that hour are Polish women on their way home from cleaning office buildings all night. They share plastic containers of pale Slavic food that you know is buttery and delicious. It's just potatoes, rice, meat, and cabbage in an endless series of combinations.

My first and only day job (so far) was at the YMCA in Evanston, Illinois. I had moved to Chicago on Halloween of 1992, pulling into Rogers Park with people whipping eggs at my dad's Pontiac in accordance with the holiday.

I had never waited tables, and my attempt to lie about that to the manager of the Skokie, Illinois, Ruby Tuesday was unsuccessful. "Where did you work?" "The Carriage House in Havertown, Pennsylvania." My more worldly friend from home had told me to make up a restaurant and give them her phone number. "Did you do hand service or tray service?" "Tray." My friend from home had told me to say "tray service" because it's easier. "What was your favorite thing about waiting tables?" My friend from home had not anticipated this question. "Um...the children. Waiting on cute kids...It was a family...restaurant." Game over. While "the children" may be a good nonsense answer for a Miss Universe contestant or a gubernatorial candidate, anyone who has ever waited tables—or simply gone to a restaurant with a child—knows that children are the soul-sucking worst. They take all the sugar packets out of the bowl, spill milk all over the place, and their wasted meals only cost five dollars, as compared to a nice booze-drinking adult to whom you might be able to up-sell a crispy onion-and-jalapeño crappetizer. I did not get the waiting job.

I applied for a job as the night box office manager of a small theater company in Boystown. The job paid about five dollars an hour for a four-hour shift, so I was surprised to find that it required a lengthy interview with the artistic director of the theater. I had a degree in drama, I explained. We talked (meaning she talked) about playwrights we (she) liked. It was between me and another girl for the job, and she needed to know what I had to offer the Tiny Pretentious Theater Company because "We like to think of ourselves as the most exciting theater company in Chicago." I tried a joke. "I like to think of myself as the most beautiful woman in the world. But where will that get either of us, really?" The other girl got the job.

My mother arranged for a friend to see me at a downtown lawyer's office for a receptionist job. I wore the electric blue polyester Hillary Clinton power suit that my roommate and I shared for such occasions. The hourlong train ride and scramble to find the exact address had made me late, and by the time I got to the interview I was sweating my roommate's BO out of the suit. The stench of every drink and every cigarette she'd had the last time she wore it filled the high-end office in which I interviewed. Between the suit, its booze cloud, and my thick virgin eyebrows, I was deemed unfit to answer phones in plain view. I was turning out to be college educated and unemployable in even the most basic way.

Thankfully, my electric-blue-suitmate was an uninhibited vagina about town. She hooked up with an early Obama prototype named Marcus who worked at the Evanston YMCA. They were looking for someone to work the front desk from 5:30 A.M. to 2:30 P.M. I got the job! Evanston is the diverse suburb just north of Chicago where Northwestern University is. The YMCA there was a great mix of a high-end yuppie fitness facility, a wonderful community resource for families, and an old-school residence for disenfranchised men. It may also have been the epicenter of all human grimness.

There was a resident named Mr. Engler who wore a wig on top of his hair like a hat. He came downstairs once a week to get his Meals on Wheels, which were left with me. I developed a *One Flew Over the Cuckoo's Nest* style of professionalism. I've always been a Zelig that way. I'm the jerk who starts to drawl when talking to Southerners and I get very butch very fast when playing organized sports. "Here we go! Hands on knees, ladies!" So when it came to the weird residents at the Y, I leaned right into the role of respectful, put-upon caregiver.

"Mr. Engler, your meals are here." He would say nothing and make no eye contact as he slid the containers toward himself with his Howard Hughes fingernails. "You have a good day, sir." I would go back to folding towels with stoic dignity, like Michael Learned on *Nurse*.

"Sir, may I see your room key?" I'd bark across the lobby like a young Betty Thomas on *Hill Street Blues*. The residents weren't allowed to have guests up in their rooms, and every now and then a guy would come in with a friend wearing a big coat and a hat and you'd realize it was a woman. These borderline-homeless guys were sneaking women up to their rooms, which only goes to show that women continue to corner the market on low gag reflex.

Not all the residents were catatonic. There was Joe the mail guy. Joe had a big white mustache and a friendly Daffy Duck speech impediment from missing teeth. He straddled the worlds of the residence and the office because he had a part-time job sorting the mail. "Morning, Joe." I'd smile like Marilu Henner in *Taxi*. "Whath's up, kid?" Joe would fire back. We'd goof on our coworkers and laugh it up at the members who gave us a hard time. All that was missing was the studio audience and an eighty-thousand-dollar-an-episode salary.

Donna worked the phones. A heavyset redheaded gal with no makeup and big fleshy hands, Donna was harder to play opposite. Generally, if she was complaining about some work situation, you could pass the time by agreeing with her, but it had to be done in a specific way. All the complaining had to be done with very few words and no dramatic flair. To rant and rave would be too show-offy. Donna would never "hold court" and you shouldn't either. Her complaints were like little WWII telegrams of bad news.

DONNA: They're making us work on Thanksgiving.

ME: No way. Are you kidding me?

DONNA: Members want to work out.

ME: That sucks. Weren't you gonna go visit your daughter in Indiana?

DONNA: Postponed.

But *do not* try to get ahead of Donna and initiate the complaining, no matter how sure you are that she'll agree. Because Donna will leave you hanging every time.

ME: Can you believe they're cutting our lunch down to half an hour, lowering our pay by ten percent, taking away our insurance, and making us eat dirt?!

DONNA: I don't go to doctors. I like dirt anyway, so … fine by me.

Donna was an enigma wrapped in bacon wrapped in a crescent roll.

One Monday, Donna came in and said that her husband

had had a heart attack over the weekend. And, by the way, she didn't open with this. She slipped it in about twenty minutes into her shift. She said her husband started having chest pains on Saturday. On their way to the ER, he made her stop at Burger King because he knew once he got to the hospital "they'd never let him have that stuff again." She didn't say anything else about it, but I covered the phones for her a couple times that day while she went to the bathroom, presumably to cry.

That's the main thing I learned in that job—how to be a considerate coworker. Cover the phones for someone so they can pee. Punch someone's time card in for them after lunch so they can stop and buy a birthday card. Help people when their register doesn't add up. Don't be a tattletale.

I'm the kind of person who likes to feel like part of a community. I will make strange bedfellows rather than have no bedfellows. In high school I had this friend for a while named Dawn. We were sitting around my house watching MTV one day when a Tina Turner video came on. On the stage behind Tina Turner was a set of giant letters spelling out TINA.

DAWN: Wow. Can you even imagine seeing your name that big?
ME: Yeah, well, that is my name.
DAWN: What? Oh. Yeah.

We could rap like that for hours.
The point is, I liked the YMCA job at first because I

wanted so desperately to like it. My day wasn't wall-to-wall grimness. The members of the gym were perfectly nice yuppies and young moms. There was a gorgeous red-headed baby I called Big Head Bob who brightened my day whenever he came in for "Toddler Gym N Stuff N Mommy N Thangs."

The Y had a preschool attached to it, and the parade of little kids coming over to swim was adorable and life affirming. I developed a crush on a shoulderless young preschool teacher named Eli. He was a complete nerd, but he had big brown eyes and he was great with the kids, and remember, when you work in what is basically a cage that you're not allowed to leave, your choices are limited to what strolls by.

Which isn't to say I didn't have any other options. I was "hit on" by a resident once. He was a forty-something white guy who was only there for a week or so. He told us all that he was in town scouting locations for a movie. I don't know what kind of movie would put their locations scout up at a YMCA, but if I had to guess I would say it was not *Titanic*. Anyway, this guy seemed almost normal until he walked up to me at the front desk, handed me a little cardboard box, said, "Voulez vous couchez avec moi?" and walked away. In the box was a packet of SweeTarts and two used Linda Ronstadt tapes. Needless to say, we married in the spring.

Eli the Preschool Teacher—which is what he'd be called if this were *Fiddler on the Roof*—was also an aspiring actor, so I invited him to come see a staged reading of a play I was in. He said yes and then showed up with his girlfriend, who was a doctor. She had about as much personality as he had shoulders.

I settled into a daily routine. Wake up at 4:40 A.M., shower, get on the train north by ten after five. Punch in by 5:30. I learned how long a morning can be. If you're at work at 5:30 A.M., five hours go by and it is 10:30 in the morning. (I didn't experience that again until I had a newborn baby. It does make you feel like an asshat for all those college years when you slept until 12:45.) At my lunch break, I'd buy a sandwich from the machine in our vendeteria. Apparently it used to be a real cafeteria with "the greatest fries," but then someone decided that wasn't quite sad enough and it was grim-ovated into a room full of vending machines.

On Fridays I might treat myself to a greasy slice of pizza and onion rings at Giggio's down the street. I'd try not to think about the fact that my seven-dollar meal was basically an hour's wages. On my way back and forth I might encounter Gregory. Gregory was a fixture around Evanston, well-known for stopping anyone on the street and telling them his story, which went like this: "Hello, my name is Gregory. I used to be an accountant. I had a lovely wife and family. I had a big house. One day I had to go to the store, but my wife had the car. I took my bike, but I didn't wear a helmet. I got hit by a truck. I suffered a head injury. I still have difficulty walking. I lost everything. My wife left me. I lost my job. So when you ride your bike, think of me and always wear a helmet." His injury had also destroyed his short-term memory, so he would tell you his story every time he met you.

When Gregory wasn't walking around town telling this story, he was coming to the Y for his daily swim. I met him every day for several months.

The people who worked upstairs in the offices would breeze by the front desk to pick up their messages. Returning from their hourlong lunches in restaurants, going to the bathroom whenever they wanted, the office people had it made. A guy in boxer shorts never screamed at them that the resident lounge TV was broken. They never got reprimanded for peeling an orange while working. Our only power over them was that we had to "buzz them in" to the front desk area, and sometimes Donna and I would buzz it too short so they'd push on the door and it was already locked again. The small joys.

The guy in charge of the residence was a big doughy bald guy whose last name had more consonants in it than I have in this book. I always thought he had the hardest job. He had to deal with all of these gentlemen and whatever their complicated, depressing backstories were. He seemed to have a lot of compassion, but he also had to be tough and kick people out sometimes.

Unlike the women who ran the fitness program or the child care program, he experienced zero point zero fun in his day-to-day work. Even at Christmas, when other departments were doing crafts with kids or having Secret Santa with their coworkers, Mr. Mczrkskczk had to organize a holiday dinner in the basement for all the men who had nowhere to go.

When I took the job at the front desk in early November, I had stipulated that I had to have off a few days around Christmas because I had already booked a flight home to see my family. This being my first Christmas after college, I was used to having a month off over the holidays, and cutting that down to a three-day weekend already had me weepy and depressed. I'm sure that I in some way screwed Donna over by doing this, and she probably ranted and raved to her husband, "Gotta work Christmas. Stop."

The twenty-third came. I punched my time card and headed out, excited to see my family and enjoy some middle-class comforts. On my way out of the building, I passed the Men's Residence Christmas Dinner. If you've ever witnessed a school bus accident or a dog trying to nudge its dead owner back to life, then the sight of this dinner probably wouldn't affect you. But for me, it was easily the third-saddest thing I've ever seen in my life.

The residents were at a long table in the basement, and Mr. Mkvcrkvckz was wearing a Santa hat with his dingy suit. There had been some kind of turkey dinner, because the place smelled like gravy, and they were just opening their presents. A tall goony kid named Timmy held up a pair of tube socks. There were tube socks for Mr. Engler. Opening tube socks over here, boss! They all got tube socks. It wasn't the tube socks that got me. It wasn't knowing that these guys would get nothing else for Christmas. It was the thought of Mr. Mvzkrskchs at the dollar store buying forty pairs of tube socks that set me weeping all the way home. This was compounded by the fact that Whitney Houston's cover of "I Will Always Love You" was constantly on my FM Walkman radio around that time. I think that made me cry because I associated it with absolutely no one.

After a visit to civilization with my family, I found the front desk harder to take.

There was a rich old guy named John Donnelly who must have donated a bunch of money. He had forgotten his member card one day, and when I tried to explain that it was a four-dollar fee to enter without a card, he went batshit. "Don't you know who I am, goddammit?" I had never seen him before. "Do you know who *I* am?" I wanted to say. "Then how could I know who *you* are? *We don't know each other.*" My boss pulled me aside and told me to just give him whatever he wanted no matter how much of a prick he was. I found he usually wanted a free guest pass for whoever was with him instead of paying the six bucks. This chiseling behavior helped me realize that most gym fees are a scam and only suckers pay them. I found myself pocketing the occasional guest-pass money and treating myself to some Giggio's. What was happening to my moral compass?

One day sweet goony Timmy came down to the lobby with a dark look in his eyes. He was pacing the lobby, ignoring us. "Heeth off his medth!" Joe Daffy-Ducked from the mail room when he saw him. "Heeth off his medth!" Joe's Daffy Duckism spread into his body as he flitted around in a panic. By the time I figured out that Joe was saying "He's off his meds," as in "off his medication," it was too late. Sweet Timmy had rushed up to a young mom in Lycra workout pants and blurted, "I wanna squirt it in your mouth." Poor Tim, he was in big trouble. Mr. Mrkkkzzz had to be called in early. The young mother was beside herself. That's the kind of trouble you get when diverse groups of people actually cross paths with one another. That's why many of the worst things in the world happen in and around Starbucks bathrooms.

I started to see a pattern at the Young Men's Christian Association. It was a power pyramid. At the bottom were all these disenfranchised residents who had to be taken care of like children, above them were a middle class of women who did all the work and kept the place running, and above them were two or three of the least-useful men you ever met. There was our comptroller, Lonny, who never once entered a room without saying, "Are we having fun yet?" He never went anywhere without food on his face. And his exit line was always "There's a million stories in the naked city." There was the program director, who talked exclusively in nonsense business language: "We are attempting to pro-activate the community by utilizing a series of directives intended to maximate communicative agreeance." At the very top of the pyramid was Executive Director Rick Chang, who had no idea who anyone was or what anyone did. He's the one who reprimanded me for peeling an orange at the front desk.

I heard from Donna that an office job was opening up in the office. "Vicky's assistant's going back to school. Stop. Think I'm gonna go for it. Stop." I was happy for Donna. Getting a job in the office would literally change her life.

I continued to be strung along by Eli No Shoulders — which is what he'd be called if this were a Native American folktale. He now claimed to have broken up with his girlfriend. I sat through a lot of Hal Hartley movies. He described his plans for a one-man show about Charlie Chaplin. Nothing came of any of it.

By the end of January, I had started taking improv classes at night. I was making new friends, actual friends who were not from planet Grim. But the classes cost money, and my 4:40 A.M. wake-up was getting harder and harder. One February morning was so cold that they closed school. There wasn't any snow; they just closed school because they didn't want kids dropping dead at the bus stop. I waited for the train at 5:10 A.M. wrapped in multiple hats and scarves so that only my eyes were exposed. By the time I got to Evanston, all the blood vessels around my eyes had burst from the temperature. I ran into Gregory. He told me his story and I assured him that I always wore a bike helmet. When I finally punched in, one of my coworkers at the front desk was giggling about something. He told me that Daffy Duck Joe was telling people that he and I were "doing it." That's what I got for engaging in simple pleasantries? A sixty-year-old hobo jerking it to me upstairs? Before I could get too worked up, Gregory was now at the front desk. As I swiped his membership card, he introduced himself to me, told me his story, and suggested I wear a bike helmet. Rising to an Irish boil behind Gregory was John Donnelly, who could not be kept waiting. "Take my card. Do you know who I am goddammit?"

Enough was enough. I was going to have to steal that office job from Donna. And that's where my college education finally gave me the unfair advantage I'd been waiting for. I wore jeans to my interview with Vicky. It was easy. Did I have basic computer skills? Sure, I was twenty-two. Did I have a good temperament on the phone? Sure. What were my career goals? "Do this job to pay for improv classes." Good enough. I went back downstairs to relieve Donna on the phones. "You're up," I told her. As I watched her nervously trundle up the steps to her interview, I knew it was no contest. Poor Donna had been at the front desk too long. You could smell other people's grimness on her, like my roommate's BO wafting out of the blue suit.

Donna would have thrown herself into that office job with deep commitment for the rest of her life. I stayed less than a year and bailed when I got a job with The Second City Touring Company.

That makes me sound like a jerk, I know. But remember the beginning of the story where I was the underdog? No? Me neither.

The Windy City,
Full of Meat

The most fun job I ever had was working at a theater in Chicago called The Second City. If you've never heard of The Second City, it is an improvisation and sketch comedy theater in Chicago, founded in 1959 by some University of Chicago brainiacs. There's a Second City theater in Chicago and one in Toronto, and between the two they have turned out some mind-blowing alumni, including John Belushi, Gilda Radner, Dan Aykroyd, Chris Farley, John Candy, Catherine O'Hara, Eugene Levy, Andrea Martin, Steve Carell, Amy Sedaris, Amy Poehler, and Stephen Colbert. I could go on, but my editor told me that was a cheap way to flesh out the book.

I moved to Chicago in 1992 to study improv and it was everything I wanted it to be. It was like a cult. People ate, slept, and definitely drank improv. They worked at crappy day jobs just to hand over their money for improv classes. Eager young people in khakis and polo shirts were willing to do whatever teachers like Del Close and Martin de Maat told them to. In retrospect, it may actually have been a cult.

I had studied legit acting methods in college—Stanislavsky, Meisner, Cicely Berry's *The Actor and His Text*—but any TV critic will tell you that I never mastered any of them. Improvisation as a way of working made sense to me. I love the idea of two actors on stage with nothing—no costumes, no sets, no dialogue—who make up something together that is then completely real to everyone in the room. The rules of improvisation appealed to me not only as a way of creating comedy, but as a worldview. Studying improvisation literally changed my life. It set me on a career path toward *Saturday Night Live*. It changed the way I look at the world, and it's where I met my husband. What has your cult done for you lately?

When I first started working at The Second City, there were two resident companies and three touring companies. The resident companies would write and perform original sketch comedy shows for packed houses in Chicago. The touring companies would take the best pieces from these shows and perform them in church basements and community centers around the country. We traveled by van to all kinds of destinations, from upstate New York to St. Paul, Minnesota, to Waco, Texas.

In the touring company we were paid seventy-five dollars per show and a twenty-five-dollar per diem. Of course, sometimes you'd have a show in Kansas followed by a show in Texas followed by another show in Kansas, so you'd have to ride in the van for two days to get to your seventy-five-dollar gig. It wasn't lucrative, but it was show business!

There were three touring companies: Red Company, Green Company, and Blue Company. I was in the Blue Company, or BlueCo as we called it to be unbelievably cool. I still feel affection for the members of BlueCo like we served in the military together. Specifically the French military, because we were lazy and a little bit sneaky. For example, they once sent us on a tour of Texas and the Midwest, and the moment the van pulled away from the theater, we all agreed to throw out the "best of" sketches we had been directed to perform and replace them with our own original material. Amy Poehler in particular was tired of being handed dated old blond-girl roles where all her lines were things like "Here's your coffee, honey," or "Mr. Johnson will see you now," or "Whattaya mean a blind date?!" Each night we'd pull out an old sketch and replace it with something of our own. My friend Ali Farahnakian, who is a genius in many ways, wrote a very funny monologue about the McDonald's Big Mac. During the course of the monologue he would eat an entire Big Mac Extra Value Meal onstage. Because the meal was technically a prop, he made the stage manager buy it for him every night and he kept his twenty-five dollars. These were the kinds of skills you learned touring for The Second City. By the time we returned to Chicago ten days later, the "best of" show was completely gone and we were in big trouble, except we didn't really care.

The Rules of Improvisation
That Will Change Your Life and Reduce Belly Fat *

*T*he first rule of improvisation is *AGREE*. Always agree and SAY YES. When you're improvising, this means you are required to agree with whatever your partner has created. So if we're improvising and I say, "Freeze, I have a gun," and you say, "That's not a gun. It's your finger. You're pointing your finger at me," our improvised scene has ground to a halt. But if I say, "Freeze, I have a gun!" and you say, "The gun I gave you for Christmas! You bastard!" then we have started a scene because we have AGREED that my finger is in fact a Christmas gun.

Now, obviously in real life you're not always going to agree with everything everyone says. But the Rule of Agreement reminds you to "respect what your partner has created" and to at least start from an open-minded place. Start with a YES and see where that takes you.

As an improviser, I always find it jarring when I meet someone in real life whose first answer is no. "No, we can't do that." "No, that's not in the budget." "No, I will not hold your hand for a dollar." What kind of way is that to live?

The second rule of improvisation is not only to say yes, but *YES, AND*. You are supposed to agree and then add something of your own. If I start a scene with "I can't believe it's so hot in here," and you just say, "Yeah..." we're kind of at a standstill. But if I say, "I can't believe it's so hot in here," and you say, "What did you expect? We're in hell." Or if I say, "I can't believe it's so hot in here," and you say, "Yes, this can't be good for the wax figures." Or if I say, "I can't believe it's so hot in here," and you say, "I told you we shouldn't have crawled into this dog's mouth," now we're getting somewhere.

* Improv will not reduce belly fat.

To me YES, AND means don't be afraid to contribute. It's your responsibility to contribute. Always make sure you're adding something to the discussion. Your initiations are worthwhile.

The next rule is MAKE STATEMENTS. This is a positive way of saying "Don't ask questions all the time." If we're in a scene and I say, "Who are you? Where are we? What are we doing here? What's in that box?" I'm putting pressure on you to come up with all the answers.

In other words: Whatever the problem, be part of the solution. Don't just sit around raising questions and pointing out obstacles. We've all worked with that person. That person is a drag. It's usually the same person around the office who says things like "There's no calories in it if you eat it standing up!" and "I felt menaced when Terry raised her voice."

MAKE STATEMENTS also applies to us women: Speak in statements instead of apologetic questions. No one wants to go to a doctor who says, "I'm going to be your surgeon? I'm here to talk to you about your procedure? I was first in my class at Johns Hopkins, so?" Make statements, with your actions and your voice.

Instead of saying "Where are we?" make a statement like "Here we are in Spain, Dracula." Okay, "Here we are in Spain, Dracula" may seem like a terrible start to a scene, but this leads us to the best rule:

THERE ARE NO MISTAKES, only opportunities. If I start a scene as what I think is very clearly a cop riding a bicycle, but you think I am a hamster in a hamster wheel, guess what? Now I'm a hamster in a hamster wheel. I'm not going to stop everything to explain that it was really supposed to be a bike. Who knows? Maybe I'll end up being a police hamster who's been put on "hamster wheel" duty because I'm "too much of a loose cannon" in the field. In improv there are no mistakes, only beautiful happy accidents. And many of the world's greatest discoveries have been by accident. I mean, look at the Reese's Peanut Butter Cup, or Botox.

Bossypants Lesson #183: You Can't Boss People Around If They Don't Really Care

The producers tried to punish BlueCo by giving us the worst gigs. Prom shows were held at one A.M. after a high school prom, and attendance was mandatory. It was basically a way to keep kids from drinking or having sex on prom night, and the performers hated doing these shows almost as much as the kids hated watching them. Imagine how mad you would be if you were missing out on a toothy knob job to watch some cult members make up a song about the 1996 election.

There were other terrible shows. Brightly lit hotel ballrooms with broken microphones. College shows where the kids were all drunk. Charity buyouts where the audience was very, very sober. Corporate gigs at eight A.M. for employees who were there to be told about reductions in their health care benefits. Basically, any time you were performing for an audience that was not there voluntarily, it was a rough show.

After seven or eight months of touring, we started to wonder which of us actors would get promoted to one of the main companies. The Mainstage cast and the "Second City e.t.c." cast got to stay in Chicago and earn a unionized living wage. They would develop their own sketches by improvising in front of an audience, then keeping the ideas that had worked until they had a full two-hour show. It was the dream job. However, of all the places I've worked that were supposedly boys' clubs, The Second City was the only one where I experienced institutionalized gender nonsense. For example, a director of one of the main companies once justified cutting a scene by saying, "The audience doesn't want to see a scene between two women." Whaaa? More on that later.

In 1995, each cast at The Second City was made up of four men and two women. When it was suggested that they switch one of the companies to three men and three women, the producers and directors had the same panicked reaction. "You can't do that. There won't be enough parts to go around. There won't be enough for the girls." This made no sense to me, probably because I speak English and have never had a head injury. We weren't doing *Death of a Salesman. We were making up the show ourselves. How could there not be enough parts?* Where was the "Yes, and"? If everyone had something to contribute, there would be enough. The insulting implication, of course, was that the women wouldn't have any ideas.

I'm happy to say the producers did jump into the twentieth century and switch to a cast of "three and three," and I got to be that third woman in the first gender-equal cast. However, I must say, as a point of pride, that I didn't get the job *because I was a woman.* I got the job because Amy Poehler had moved to New York with the Upright Citizens Brigade and I was the next best thing.

But this was the first time I experienced what I like to call "The Myth of Not Enough."

When I worked at *Saturday Night Live,* I had a five A.M. argument with one of our most intelligent actresses. It was rumored that Lorne was adding another woman to the cast, and she was irate. (In fairness, she was also exhausted. It was five A.M. after writing all night.) She felt there wouldn't be enough for the girls and that this girl was too similar to her. There wouldn't be enough screen time to go around.

I revived my old argument: How could this be true if *we made up the show?* A bunch of us suggested that they collaborate instead of compete. And, of course, that's what they did, with great success, once they were actually in a room together. But where does that initial panic come from?

This is what I tell young women who ask me for career advice. People are going to try to trick you. To make you feel that you are in competition with one another. "You're up for a promotion. If they go with a woman, it'll be between you and Barbara." Don't be fooled. You're not in competition with other women. You're in competition with *everyone.*

Also, I encourage them to always wear a bra. Even if you don't think you need it, just... you know what? You're never going to *regret* it.

My dream for the future is that sketch comedy shows become a gender-blind meritocracy of whoever is really the funniest. You might see four women and two men. You might see five men and a YouTube video of a kitten sneezing. Once we know we're really open to all the options, we can proceed with Whatever's the Funniest... which will probably involve farts.

My Honeymoon, or A Supposedly Fun Thing I'll Never Do Again Either*

My husband doesn't like to fly. He *does* fly now because he doesn't want our daughter to grow up thinking he is a Don Knotts character. But when we were first married, he didn't fly.

I made him fly once before we were married because

---

* If you get this reference to David Foster Wallace's 1997 collection of essays, consider yourself a member of the cultural elite. Why do you hate your country and flag so much?!

he was offered a free trip to Vienna, Austria, to direct a sketch comedy show for an English-language theater. If you know anything about Vienna, you know that they love Chicago-style sketch comedy!*

Anyway, not knowing then the depth of his fear, I bullied him into taking the free trip to Austria, assuring him that I would be with him all the way and talk him through the flight. To get to Vienna from Chicago, you fly to Zurich, drop through the bumpy air pockets around the Alps, land, and then take off again. This is the worst thing for fearful flyers because they all cling to that same fact nugget like Rain Man: "Most planes crash during takeoff and landing!" We were doing twice as much taking off and landing as he had agreed to. This was unacceptable. He was miserable the entire week we were there, distracted by worry about the trip home.

I swore I would never make him fly again.

Just years later, we get married. Marriage leads to a honeymoon, which traditionally involves travel.

For our honeymoon, we book a cruise to Bermuda because the ship leaves from New York. (We don't have to fly to Miami to get on it.) We board the ship from a giant hangar on the West Side of Manhattan. There are guys playing steel drums and handing you drinks. They don't ask if you are a recovering alcoholic or if you are on any medications that might interact negatively with alcohol. This is maritime law! You get a drink without asking.

---

* The Viennese do not enjoy American sketch comedy.

After a brief "muster drill" where no one pays attention to where their lifeboat station is, the fun begins. And the first few days are pretty fun.

We have a little room with a balcony. The couple next door has a balcony about ten inches away. They don't introduce themselves, but they are comically drunk most of the time and the wife wears a spangly American-flag bikini, leading me to believe she is a retired stripper.

There's a pool, kind of. It's more like a big sloshing kiddie pool, and if you get in it, you feel like you are taking a bath with strangers.

There are some wonderful Filipinos who fold your towels in the shape of a different animal every night. It might be an elephant wearing your sunglasses, or a duck wearing your sunglasses. It's just fun. Don't overthink it.

There are fun activities hosted by our cruise director, who calls himself "Dan Dan the Party Man." He has recently replaced the previous cruise director, "Pete Pete the Party Meat," who replaced "Guy Guy the Funtimes Person," who had recently died of autoerotic asphyxiation. No, that part's not true! That's a joke-lie. I'm not going to lie to you in this story because I want you to know that the rest of it is true.

Dan Dan the Party Man leads poolside games that include: People pretending to be horses in a steeplechase. A dance contest. Something with beach balls.

At mealtimes we sit at an assigned table. The other two couples at our table are middle-aged in-laws from the Delaware Water Gap. Richard and Barbra, Betty and Bernie.

We talk about dog breeds and fishing; my knowledge of both topics is equal. We agree that the ship's food is as good as any restaurant in New York (between 48th and 50th Street on Seventh Avenue). Betty and Bernie say they wanted to take this trip as a do-over of their honeymoon. Apparently, they had honeymooned in Bermuda thirty-five years ago and the whole trip had been a disaster because Betty broke her arm falling off a scooter. "Never rent a scooter in Bermuda," Bernie says. Betty overlaps him, "They always tell you on these cruises, don't rent a scooter when you get to Bermuda. You're not used to it. You'll have an accident. But people don't listen." We all agree; people just don't listen.

While our little six-top gets along fine, we are all silently jealous of nearby table twenty, a mix of young couples and stray gays who are hitting it off big-time. Every lull in our discussion of "German shepherds we have known" is filled with a boisterous drunken laugh from table twenty.

It is worth noting that at this time, I had been doing Weekend Update on *Saturday Night Live* for two full seasons. I am not recognized by anyone. Well, I *am* recognized by the guy who refills the soft-serve ice cream machine by the pool, but not for being on TV, just for lingering. For O! The desserts! Rows and rows of pastries laid out cafeteria-style. Some of them are unidentifiable squares of pink stuff. I think we called it junket back in the seventies. They don't taste good; but like a schoolboy at his first coed dance, I am drawn not so much by their beauty as by their unlimited quantities.

On day three I am very excited to attend one of our special excursions for which you pay extra. We are going to get off the boat early in the morning in Bermuda, where we will be given bicycles. We will ride our bikes around the island with a guide to a special secluded beach where we can swim and have rum swizzles and then we will be taken back to the ship by a party boat. Sounds pretty good, right? That's what I thought, too. I wouldn't shut up about it. For weeks before we left I bragged about how I had chosen the best excursion. It was fun and fitness combined! It was a great way to see the island! My husband and I wait at the designated pickup point at 8:30 A.M. No one else shows up. A quick check of our itinerary reveals the heartbreaking truth. The bike trip was yesterday. In my excitement, I memorized it wrong. I cry. I cry like a three year old who just wants to take her toy cash register into the bathtub. I cry in a way that reveals that I'm not finding the rest of the cruise that fun.

This is definitely the low point of the trip, until the fire. Oh yes, there's a ship fire coming in this story. Wait for it.

Once my fitness-and-fun dreams are dashed, I start to lean hard into the food. Soft serve, hot dog time at the pool, a nightly aperitif called the Chocolate Mudslide, which is basically a twenty-ounce chocolate shake with a thimble of Bailey's in it.

The last night of the cruise is formal night. My husband, who for legal reasons I will call Barry, is wearing a suit that he had custom-made for him by a Portuguese tailor in Pennsylvania. I am wearing a dress that was foisted on me by some aggressive Russian salespeople on the Upper West Side of Manhattan. Needless to say, we are feeling very continental. Photographers come to the tables and take formal photos of us all, as well as novelty photos of us being menaced tableside by a woman dressed as a pirate. During dinner there is a passenger talent show. And sure enough, the little gay from table twenty does a tap dance, cheered on by his new best friends. Those assholes.

After dinner we settle into the ship's thousand-seat theater to enjoy the eleven P.M. performance of Fiesta Caliente. The house is packed for this musical dance celebration of Latin pop music. One of the dancers is "warming up" on stage as part of the preshow, a theatrical convention that my husband and I can appreciate because we're from New York and know about things. My Chocolate Mudslide is going down smooth when we hear the three bells. *Bing. Bing. Bing.* But instead of Dan Dan the Party Man, it's a woman's voice and she's breathing heavily. She sounds Filipina, if that's even a thing. "Bravo...Bravo...Bravo," she pants. "Main engine. Starboard side. Bravo...Bravo... Bravo." We hear the speaker shut off. People look around a little nervously. The dancer warming up on stage makes a beeline for backstage. Within seconds the three bells are back. Oh, thank God, it's our Greek captain. "Laydis and gentlemen, thissis your captain spicking. Pliss proceed to your muster stations." This is not what I wanted him to say. We get up and make our way painfully slowly through the completely full theater.

Everyone is quiet. Which is the wooooooorst. It's scary when a group of people all know instinctively not to joke around. Another voice comes over the PA, repeating, "Please, remain calm. Please proceed to your muster stations." The German half of me is thinking, "Shove the old people out of the way. Shove the old and the infirm! If they are strong enough to resist you, they deserve to live." The Greek half of me wants to scream at our Greek captain. I do neither and proceed obediently.

We stop at our cabin along the way so that I can change into sneakers. I have a strong urge to lie down and pretend this is not happening—like the old couple in *Titanic*. That's how I want to go, ice-cold water rising around our spooning bodies and me somehow successfully willing my body to nap. I tie my Sauconys.* "We should hurry," Jeff says quietly. (Damnit, I promised myself I wouldn't use his real name!) We head to our muster station, grateful that we went to the drill. Women and children are put to the front, men in the back. They really still do that. I hold Jeff's hand diagonally through the crowd. We're going to be one of those stories of a couple that died on their honeymoon. We'll be on the local news. They'll identify Jeff by the monogram inside that suit jacket. I think about how horrible it will be if I have to get on the lifeboat and leave him behind.

Another announcement. "This is Dan your cruise director. We have a fire in the engine room due to a burst

* This is a paid endorsement from the Saucony Corporation.

fuel pipe. Our crew is working hard to put the fire out, and I will update you as I have more information." Uh-oh. Where's Dan Dan the Party Man?

I look around. There are several tween-age girls, in tears, girls who have no doubt watched *Titanic* more times than you have looked at your own stools. There are littler kids who are laughing, unaware. There are the dopes who broke their arms and ankles on scooters (people really don't listen), who are now wondering if it will cost them their lives. The wildly drunk man from the cabin next door to ours is in front of me in the crowd. He's so drunk that he's standing in the women-and-children section. He complains loudly that this is boring and that we are a bunch of assholes. When a clearly terrified woman blurts out, "Please, sir, be quiet," he sways for a second and then lets out a long "Shuuuuut uuuuuuup" that is funny not just because of its Jackie Gleason–style delivery but also because of its inappropriateness in a situation where we're all probably going to die.

About thirty minutes later, Dan Dan the Death Man comes back on, saying that thanks to the excellent work of the firefighters on the crew, the fire is out. We will be able to return to our cabins as soon as the rest of the ship has been checked. He says the heat from the fire set off every fire alarm on the ship and so every chamber must be checked before we can go back inside. Most people take this as good news. But I'm too smart for that. I know that extreme heat plus a burst fuel pipe means that the ship is going to explode now. While people around me start to relax, I keep my eyes on the sea, waiting to be rocketed into it on a wave of fire. I'll be ready for it to happen and that way it won't happen. It's a burden, being able to control situations with my hyper-vigilance, but it's my lot in life.

Some crew members come around with coolers of cold drinks. A nearby woman takes a soda and hands it back, saying, "Do you have diet?" If God had a sense of humor, the ship would have exploded right then. (Actually, I think God does have a sense of humor, as evidenced by squirrels eating pizza with their hands and that thing where suicide bombers accidentally detonate before they get to their destination.) The ship doesn't explode.

After an hour or so, we're allowed into the lounge and they give out playing cards. People are sleeping on the floor. It's very *Poseidon Adventure*. It's almost three A.M. when we return to our cabin. Our sunglasses are just sitting there on the bed; whatever towel animal was wearing them has fled in terror.

We sleep in our clothes. In the morning, my husband, who for legal reasons I will now call Lee, wakes me up and says that we have turned back to Bermuda. This is one of the things I love about Lee, that he is manly and old-fashioned enough to know that the sun should be on our right if we're headed north. They must be taking us back to Bermuda and flying us home. Lee's face shrinks with worry. I think about our tablemates who had mentioned they also didn't like to fly. Most of the people on this ship are afraid to fly. My God: *That's why they're here.* Cruising itself is not actually fun! I spring into action. There must be a finite amount of anti-anxiety medication on this ship. While most people are still asleep, I find the infirmary and procure two pills for my husband. One for when the plane takes off and one for when I tell him he's right, we're being sent home on a plane.

After handing the first pill to my husband, Rod (Jeff's complaining that Lee sounds too feminine. Dammit, I used his real name again!), I head to the business center and make a forty-dollar ship-to-shore call to let my parents know that in spite of what they have seen on the news, we're okay. I am surprised to learn that this was not a news story.

The crew tries to downplay the seriousness of the night before. The "midnight cooking demonstration," cancelled last night, is now being held in the hot sunlight. The guys are back playing the steel drums by the pool bar, but now the music seems creepy, like when children sing in a horror movie or when guys play steel drums on a cruise ship that almost sank. The crew is glum. The scuttlebutt (which actually is scuttlebutt and not gossip, because we're on a ship) is that the ship is being taken back to Bermuda, where it will be dry-docked and repaired for six months. No wonder they're a little halfhearted about the cooking demonstration; they're all out of a job.

I buy our formal-night picture from the photo center. That I actually pay for it, instead of just taking it after all this nonsense, is a credit to my parents. Rod and I are looking tan and grinning at the lady pirate between us.

What amount of revisionism will be necessary for this photo to be an accurate memento of our trip?

I run into Betty, Bernie, Barbra, and Richard in the cafeteria. Betty and Bernie have officially given up on Bermuda. Richard is ashen. I can tell he is the one who's terrified to fly. "Did you get some pills?" I ask. "They were out," his wife answers.

As the ship pulls back into King's Wharf, local women and children are cheering us in. Little topless boys are waving their T-shirts in the air. Nothing gives you a fear flashback like a bunch of strangers cheering in surprise that you're not dead.

They put us on a chartered flight back to New York. If you've never been on a chartered flight full of people who are afraid to fly who have also been traumatized in the past twelve hours, I recommend it more than a cruise. It's pretty funny. Everyone is jittery, and when the pilot makes the unfortunate choice of testing the PA system by saying, "Bravo, bravo," you can almost hear people's b-holes tighten. A collective cartoon-mouse squeak of b-hole.

What if I told you now that the plane crashed while taxiing on the runway? It didn't. We made it home, shaken but tan.

The most interesting thing I learned from this trip came when I told the story to my friend James, who had been a performer on a cruise ship years before. When I told him the woman said, "Bravo, bravo, bravo," James froze. Did she really say it three times? he needed to know. Then James laid it out for me. Bravo is serious. The more times they say it, the more serious it is. The most times they ever say it is four times, and if they say it four times, it means you're going down to your watery grave. So "Bravo, bravo, bravo" was not terrific. Interesting fact number two: In the event of an emergency, it is the entertainers who are in charge of the lifeboats. Because the rest of the crew has actual nautical duties, the kids from Fiesta Caliente are trained to man the lifeboats. If you ever have to get on a lifeboat, the person in charge of your safety will likely be a nineteen-year-old dancer from Tampa who just had a fight with his boyfriend about the new Rihanna video. James also told me that each lifeboat has a gun on it and that once a lifeboat is in the water, the performer–lifeboat captain is trained to shoot anyone who is disruptive. This is apparently legal in accordance with maritime law.

About a week later, we get a letter of apology in the mail offering us a free cruise of equal or lesser value as compensation this offer is non-transferable. I'm pretty sure the only people who took that offer were the drunk guy next door, his stripper wife, and those dicks from table twenty. But I shall not cruise again. Luxury cruises were designed to make something unbearable—a two-week transatlantic crossing—seem bearable. There's no need to do it now. There are planes. You wouldn't take a vacation where you ride on a stagecoach for two months but there's all-you-can-eat shrimp. You wouldn't take a vacation where you have an old-timey appendectomy without anesthesia while steel drums play. You *might* take a vacation where you ride on a camel for two days if they gave you those animal towels wearing your sunglasses.

"What were you thinking when we were holding hands diagonally?" I ask. Jeff says, "I was thinking, 'It's going to be so hard for her when she chooses not to get on that lifeboat and stay with me.'"

I decide I can't start this marriage with a lie.

"Really?" I say. "'Cause I was thinking that it was going to be so hard for you when I got on the lifeboat and you had to stay behind." He is appalled. I plead my case. "Remember when we saw *Titanic* how mad I was at Kate Winslet when she climbed out of the lifeboat and back onto the ship? I think she encumbered Leonardo DiCaprio. If she had gone on the lifeboat, then he could have had that piece of wood she was floating on and they both would have survived. I would never do that to you."

I wait for his response, hoping that in the twenty-first century romantic love can be defined as not lying about your plans to get on the lifeboat and remembering to get your partner some pills. He just laughs. With that settled, we begin our married life.

The Secrets of
Mommy's Beauty

I know why you bought this book. Or should I say, I know why you borrowed this book from that woman at your office. You want to know my secret beauty regimen. I learned early on that a woman must master and protect the "Secrets of Her Beauty," but I will share with you my Twelve Tenets of Looking Amazing Forever.

1) Form Good Beauty Habits Early

"How do you stay so eternally youthful?" "Your skin is so flawless. What's your secret?" people always ask Sharon Stone. Like my peer Sharon Stone, I have always felt that the simplest products are the best. Sharon credits her good skin to Pond's cold cream (and maybe a little bit of nature's own botulism. Wink!). In my youth I washed daily with Ivory soap and Prell shampoo. Everyone knew Prell was the best shampoo because you could also use it to clean a frying pan. I then dried my hair with a Hot Comb. The Hot Comb was a small vibrating, wheezing hairbrush that for some reason my family kept in the dining room credenza. Maybe it wanted to be close to the electric knife, since they were almost the exact same machine.

If I didn't have the time for the full hot-comb treatment—for example, if I was in a hurry to get outside and choreograph a pretend Pepsi commercial with my friend Maureen—I would stand in front of our giant air conditioner and let it blast my hair dry.

2) The Right Undergarments Are an Essential Part of Your Silhouette

I developed breasts very early, around nine years old. I developed breasts so weird and high, it's possible they were above my collarbone. At that point, wearing a bra was not so much about holding the breasts up, as clarifying that they were not a goiter.

My mother knew the importance of getting the right fit for a bra, so she took me to JCPenney and tried one on over my clothes. *She tried a bra on me over my clothes in the middle of JCPenney.* I thank her for this. This early breast-related humiliation prevented me from ever needing to participate in "Girls Gone Wild" in my twenties.

3) Skin Care, Skin Care, Skin Care!

Makeup companies like to make skin care seem complicated, but let me demystify it for you. The Three Secrets of Great Skin are Moisture, SOOTS (Stay Out of the Sun), and Be Italian. The Three Rules of SOOTS are Sunscreen, AWAH (Always Wear a Hat), and DLO (Don't Lay

Out). "Don't Lay Out" is a mnemonic device for "Do Lots of Omega 3s," which can be found in SWaWB (Salmon, Walnuts, and Weird Bread).

Consistency is the most important part of skin care, followed by Water Drinking, and both of those are less important than SLEEP (Sleep Like Everyone Else, Please).

At the tender age of fourteen I was already invigorating my skin with a rigorous daily massage. I squeezed and picked at every pore, harvesting any and all goo balls. This, followed by a bracing splash of Sea Breeze, has helped keep my pores large and supple to this day.

By nineteen, I had discovered that Retin-A was a great way to have large chunks of your skin peel off and waft to the floor during acting class.

4) Don't Be Afraid to Try "Outside the Box" Skin Care Solutions

I spent most of 1990 bargaining with God that I would take one gigantic lifelong back zit in exchange for clear skin on my face. While this never worked out, I do not at all regret the time I spent pursuing it. It's about the journey, people.

5) The Eyes Are the Windows to Where the Soul Is Supposed to Be

I taught Monica Lewinsky everything she knows... about eye cream. I guess I should back up and explain that. In the spring of 1999, I participated in a secret meeting with Monica Lewinsky, *SNL* producer Marci Klein, and fellow *SNL* writer Paula Pell. Marci called and asked how quickly Paula and I could get down to her Tribeca apartment. Monica Lewinsky was coming over and we three were going to convince her to appear on *SNL*. This was before Ms. Lewinsky's infamous Barbara Walters interview aired. None of us had even heard her speak before. She was still that enigmatic girl in the beret who didn't get to the dry cleaners very often.

We spent the afternoon drinking wine and eating wasabi peas. (We didn't even buy the girl lunch! Who did we think we were, presidents?) Monica was bright and personable and very open with us — maybe too open for a person in her situation. I'm just saying, Linda Tripp might not have been the intelligence-gathering mastermind you thought she was.

We talked about thongs, Weight Watchers, and Brazilian bikini waxes. (But you probably knew all that when I said it was *1999*.) When the topic turned to eye cream, I wanted to talk, so I shared the one piece of information I'd retained from the mean woman at the La Mer counter in Saks. "You're supposed to gently pat it on with your ring finger." I demonstrated. "Oh, really?" Monica asked with a level of interest and gullibility that explained a lot. To this day, I think of Monica whenever I apply my eye cream. And I'm sure she thinks of me.

6) Space Lasers

As you age, you may want to pay someone to shoot lasers at your face. If you are a fancy lady and live in a fancy urban center like New York or Dallas–Fort Worth, you go to a fancy dermatologist and they cover your eyes and point various machines at your face to "promote collagen production." If you live far from a city, you can simulate the experience at home by having a friend hide your wallet while you sit close to a space heater. It will work just as well.

For a while I was getting my "laser money removal" done by a fancy doctor on Park Avenue. One day I went to see about some hormonal acne that wouldn't go away on my jawline. The doctor eagerly injected the spot with steroids, and within a day or two the blemish had shrunk down to normal. Unfortunately, the steroids caused the spot to keep shrinking, and by the end of the week I had a divot in my jaw through which I could feel the bone. I was furious and complaining about it in the makeup chair at *SNL*. "My face is already pretty banged up and now I have *another* scar to deal with?!" Amy Poehler called to me from across the room, "The difference is…now you're *paying* for it." She was right. I really had made it. We high-fived about it later.

7) **"A Woman's Hair Is Her Crowning Glory"** — the guys who wrote the Bible

Beauty experts in the 1970s declared the shag the "most universally flattering haircut." The short layers in the front framed the face while irregular longer pieces in the back elongated the neck. I think this picture proves them right.

Finding a hairstylist you trust is key. For many years I worked exclusively with the students at the Gordon Phillips Beauty Academy. The sign out front said it all—"Gordon Phillips Beauty Academy, London, Paris, Upper Darby." Always on the cutting edge of beauty, I believe this haircut was executed by folding my face in half and cutting out a heart. Of course I must be honest; this is clearly a professional photo taken on "picture day." I didn't look this sleek and pulled together all the time.

8) **Q: But Tina, Most of Us Don't Have Constant Access to a Hairstylist. What Do We Do?**

A: First of All, Don't Speak to Me in That Tone. Second of All, You Must Learn to Tame Your Own Mane!

I first found a system that worked for me in the mid-eighties. Once or twice a week I would set my alarm for six A.M. so I could get up and plug in the Hot Stix. Hot Stix were heated rubber sticks, and you would twist your hair around them and roll it up. After about fifteen minutes, you took all the sticks out, and your hair was curled up in tight rings (with dry raggedy ends). I would study the curls in the mirror, impressed with both the appliance and my newfound ability to use it.

Then, without fail, at the last second before leaving for school, I would ask myself, "Am I supposed to brush it out or leave it?" *Why could I never remember?* That feeling of "I'm pretty sure this next step is wrong, but I'm just gonna do it anyway" is part of the same set of instincts that makes me such a great cook.

On some level I knew I wasn't supposed to brush it out, but I couldn't stop myself.

My hand — gripping the brush like it was a hand transplant from a murderer who hated beauty! — brushed through the curls, turning them into a giant static-filled mess. By the end of homeroom it was pulled into a ponytail, which really works on me, so there you have it.

Right after I graduated high school I decided to cut my hair off. This was my chance to reinvent myself before college.

After a harsh disagreement over the ideational hollowness of sausage curls, my mother and I had ended our artistic experiment with the Gordon Phillips Academy. We were now getting our hair cut by my classmate's mom, who was also a professional Ann Jillian look-alike. Yes, the feeling you're experiencing right now is jealousy. The whole family was glamorous that way. I always envied their lives because they seemed like they were living in a sitcom. They were all blond and good-looking. The mom cut hair out of her basement salon and Ann Jillian–ed part-time. You could sell this show to CBS just with that! The dad ran a restaurant. Their uncle was our school's "cool" English teacher. The oldest son was a young Bon Jovi type who was the star of our high school choir and went *all the way to New York* once a week for private hard-rock vocal coaching. The middle son was a brilliant, funny, cuddly giant who drew sardonic cartoons in the margins of things, and the baby of the family was the Jason Priestley–level adorable kid who, clearly, the producers of the family had added in the last season to boost ratings. I mean, just looking at this family, you knew they were going to make it to syndication.

It was natural that I would trust Mrs. Doyle to transform me into my new college self. I wanted to cut it all off. Not the coward's move, not a *bob:* the full choppery. Mrs. Doyle put my hair into a thick ponytail, cut that ponytail off, and handed it to me. I still have it somewhere in a cardboard box in my parents' house. I know because my mom has been politely asking me to "maybe spend an hour going through those boxes" for over twenty years now.

The haircut was cropped close on the sides, fuller on top, with two long Liza Minnelli–esque wisps that hung down like peyes. I loved it. Then I asked whether we needed the wisps, but once it was explained to me that they were mandatory, I went back to loving it.

Nerd no more, this new cut let people see the real me that was inside—a mother of four who was somehow also a virgin.

9) When It Comes to Fashion, Find What Works for You and Stick with It

A wise friend once told me, "Don't wear what fashion designers tell you to wear. Wear what *they* wear." His point being that most designers, no matter what they throw onto the runway, favor simple, flattering pieces for themselves.

Anyone who has never met me can tell you that fashion has always been very very very very very very very important to me. For example, I once told my cousin that my dream would be "if the whole store Express was my closet!" How prescient, because now, of course, I wear nothing but Express.

It can't be said enough. Don't concern yourself with fashion; stick to simple pieces that flatter your body type.

By nineteen, I had found my look. Oversize T-shirts, bike shorts, and wrestling shoes. To prevent the silhouette from being too baggy, I would cinch it at the waist with my fanny pack. I was pretty sure I would wear this look forever. The shirts allowed me to express myself with cool sayings like "There's No Crying in Baseball" and "Universität Heidelberg," the bike shorts showed off my muscular legs, and the fanny pack held all my trolley tokens. I was nailing it on a daily basis. Find something like this for yourself as soon as possible.

10) A Manicure Is a Must

Once I moved to New York in 1997, I discovered the joys of the quickie Korean manicure. The city is filled with tiny storefront nail salons where you can get a manicure-pedicure, an underarm wax, and a ten-minute series of punches in the back, all for under a hundred dollars. The first few times you go, it can be intimidating. For starters, you may forget that you yourself speak English. You enter, smile, and nod at the manager. "Manicure-pedicure?" "Pick color," she chirps back in her Korean accent. You pick out a couple of the three hundred shades of off-white. "This for manicure. This feet. Magazine okay?" *Why are you talking like that?* Now that you've racially embarrassed yourself, you are ready to squeeze into a seat at a tiny table and basically hold hands with a stranger for twenty minutes. That really is the craziest thing the first few times you go, getting used to passively flopping your hands into another woman's hands. It's like something they'd make you do at summer camp as a trust-building exercise, I assume. I never went to summer camp, as I was neither underprivileged nor Jewish nor extremely Christian nor obese. (It would be a great exercise for someone who thinks they want to move to New York. Sit in an enclosed space full of fumes and hold hands with a stranger for twenty minutes while everyone around you speaks a language you don't understand. If you enjoy this, you will enjoy the 6 train.)

To take your mind off how weird it is to have someone else clean your fingers, there is a series of theatrical performances all around you. To your right you might find a New Yorker speaking animatedly about an apartment she has seen. "It was *sick*. You don't even know. *Marble slabs*." The more New Yorkers like something, the more disgusted they are. "The kitchen was all Sub-Zero: I want to kill myself. The building has a playroom that makes you want to break your own jaw with a golf club. I can't take it." To your left may sit an older woman eating cashews with one hand while talking on the phone with the other while still receiving a manicure and oversharing. "I know. I was crying about it on the toilet this morning — [to manicurist] don't cut the cuticles, please." As you listen closer, you will suspect that she is participating in a paid therapy session over the phone. "Well, you know, it's about setting boundaries. He has to be told, 'If we're gonna have these conversations it shouldn't be when one of us is drunk and the other one is hanging upside down in the gravity boots.'" As you listen longer, you're not sure if she's the patient or the therapist. "Do I think it's *good* that you're angry? Why would I think it's good that you're angry?" There are never fewer than eight Tracey Ullman characters in any NYC nail salon at any given time.

If all this becomes too much for you, just look up and focus on the poster of a hand with long red nails holding a violin incorrectly.

Before you know it, your manicure is done and looking great. Your fingernails look healthy and fresh, and the shiny varnish will help hide the little particles of garbage and human feces that all city dwellers are slightly covered in!

11) **Aging Naturally Without Looking Like Time-Lapse Photography of a Rotting Sparrow**

At a certain point your body wants to be disgusting. While your teens and twenties were about identifying and emphasizing your "best features," your late thirties and forties are about fighting back decay. You pluck your patchy beard daily. Your big toe may start to turn jauntily inward. Overnight you may grow one long straight white pubic hair. Not that this has happened to me, of course, because every six months I get a *very* expensive Japanese treatment that turns my pubic hair clear like rice noodles.

We all mentally prepare ourselves for wrinkles, but wrinkles are not the problem. It's the unexpected grosseries.

For example, your mouth. Dear God, your mouth. No matter how diligent you are about brushing and flossing — which is never diligent enough for that show-off dental hygienist of yours — at some point you start waking up every day with a mouth that smells like a snail left in the sun. You can fix it as soon as you get up — you brush and use mouthwash — but there's something about knowing you woke up with hot-mothball mouth that makes you feel old.

I think God designed our mouths to die first to help us slowly transition to the grave. But I am a big believer in "Intelligent Design," and by that I mean I love IKEA!

12) The Most Important Rule of Beauty

If you retain nothing else, always remember the most important Rule of Beauty. "Who cares?"

Remembrances of
Being Very Very Skinny

For a brief time at the turn of the century, I was very
skinny. This is what I remember about that period.

- I was cold all the time.
- I had a pair of size-four corduroy short shorts. That
  I wore. To work. In the middle of Manhattan.
- I loved it when people told me I was getting too
  thin.
- I once took a bag of sliced red peppers to the beach
  as a snack.
- I regularly ate health food cookies so disgusting that
  when I enthusiastically gave one to Rachel Dratch she
  drew a picture of a rabbit and broke the cookie into a
  trail of tiny pieces coming out of the rabbit's butt.
- Men I had met before suddenly paid attention to
  me . . . and I hated them for it.
- Sometimes I had to sleep with a pillow between my
  legs because my bony knees clanking together kept
  me awake.

- I had a lot of time on my hands because I wasn't constantly eating.
- I ran three miles a day on a treadmill six days a week.
- I felt wonderfully superior to everyone.
- I didn't have a kid yet.

We should leave people alone about their weight. Being skinny for a while (provided you actually eat food and don't take pills or smoke to get there) is a perfectly fine pastime. Everyone should try it once, like a super-short haircut or dating a white guy.

Remembrances of Being
a Little Bit Fat

For a brief time at the end of that last century I was over-weight. This is what I remember about that period.

- My boobs were bigger.
- I once left a restaurant in the middle of dessert to get to Krispy Kreme before it closed.
- Even though I only liked McDonald's fries, I believed it was more nutritious to make a meal of it and have two cheeseburgers as well.
- If I was really ambitious, I would get a Whopper Jr. at Burger King and then walk to McDonald's to get the fries. The shake could be from anywhere.
- I could not run a mile.
- I wore oversize men's overalls that I *loved*.
- Guys who were friends with me did not want to date me . . . and I hated them for it.
- On at least three occasions, I vomited on Christmas Eve from mixing chocolate, peel-and-eat shrimp,

summer sausage, and cheese. No alcohol was involved.

- As a size twelve, I took pride in the idea that I was "real woman"–sized. "Size twelve is the national average," I would boast, "no matter what magazines try to tell you."
- Once, while ironing in my underwear, I grazed my protruding belly with the hot iron.

We should leave people alone about their weight. Being chubby for a while (provided you don't give yourself diabetes) is a natural phase of life and nothing to be ashamed of. Like puberty or slowly turning into a Republican.

A Childhood Dream, Realized

(Not the One Where I'm Being Chased
by Count Chocula)

In 1997 I flew to New York from Chicago to interview for a writing position at *Saturday Night Live*. It seemed promising because I'd heard the show was looking to diversify. Only in comedy, by the way, does an obedient white girl from the suburbs count as diversity. I came for my job interview in the only decent clothes I had—my "show clothes" from The Second City. Black pants and a lavender chenille sweater from Contempo Casuals. I went to the security guard at the elevator and I heard myself say, "I'm here to see Lorne Michaels." I couldn't believe the words that were coming out of my mouth. "I'm here to see Lorne Michaels." I was living one of my dreams. This must be how people feel when they really do go to school naked by accident.

I went up to the seventeenth-floor offices, which were lined with archival photos from the show—Jane Curtin ripping her shirt open on Weekend Update, Gilda Radner and Candice Bergen in a *Beach Blanket Bingo* sketch, Al

Franken's head shot! Then I sat on a couch and waited for my meeting with Lorne. About an hour into the wait, the assistants started making popcorn in a movie theater popcorn machine — something I would later learn signaled Lorne's imminent arrival. To this day the smell of fresh popcorn causes me to experience stress, hunger, and sketch ideas for John Goodman.

The only advice anyone had given me about meeting with Lorne was "Whatever you do, don't finish his sentences." A Chicago actress I knew had apparently made that mistake and she believed it cost her the job. When I was eventually ushered into his office, I sat down, determined not to blow it. Lorne said, "So you're from..."

It seemed to hang there forever. Why wasn't he finishing the question? If I answered now, would this count as my talking over him? I couldn't remember how normal human speech patterns worked. Another five seconds went by, and still no more sentence from Lorne. Oh, God. When I flew back to Chicago the next day they were going to say, "How was your meeting with Lorne Michaels?" And I would reply, "He said 'So you're from' and then we sat there for an hour and then a girl came in and asked me to leave."

After what was probably, realistically, ten seconds, I couldn't take it anymore and I blurted out, "Pennsylvania. I'm from Pennsylvania, a suburb of Philadelphia," just as Lorne finally finished his thought, "Chicago." I was sure I had blown it. I don't remember anything else that happened in the meeting because I just kept staring at the nameplate on his desk that said "Lorne Michaels" and thinking, "This is the guy with the Beatles check!" I couldn't believe I was in his office. I could have never guessed that in a few years I'd be sitting in that office at two, three, four in the morning, thinking, "If this meeting doesn't end soon, I'm going to kill this Canadian bastard." Somehow, I had gotten the job.

During my nine years at *Saturday Night Live,* my relationship with Lorne transitioned from "Terrified Pupil and Reluctant Teacher" to "Small-Town Girl and Streetwise Madam Showing Her the Ropes" to "Annie and Daddy Warbucks (touring company)" to one of mutual respect and friendship. Then it transitioned to "Sullen Teenage Girl and Generous Stepfather," then to "Mr. and Mrs. Michael Jackson," then, for a brief period, to "Boy Who Doesn't Believe in Christmas and Recluse Neighbor Who Proves that Miracles Are Possible," then back to mutual respect and friendship again.

I've learned many things from Lorne, in particular a managerial style that was the opposite of Bossypants.

Things I Learned from Lorne Michaels

1) "Producing is about discouraging creativity."

A TV show comprises many departments—Costumes, Props, Talent, Graphics, Set Dressing, Transportation. Everyone in every department wants to show off their skills and contribute creatively to the show, which is a blessing. You're grateful to work with people who are talented and enthusiastic about their jobs. You would think that as a producer, your job would be to churn up creativity, but mostly your job is to police enthusiasm. You may have an occasion where the script calls for a bran muffin on a white plate and the Props Department shows up with a bran cake in the shape of Santa Claus sitting on a silver platter that says "Welcome to Denmark." "We just thought it would be funny." And you have to find a polite way to explain that the character is Jewish, so her eating Santa's face might have negative connotations, and the silver tray, while beautiful, is giving a weird glare on camera and maybe let's go with the bran muffin on the white plate.

And then sometimes Actors have what they call "ideas." Usually it involves them talking more, or, in the case of more experienced actors, sitting more. When Actors have ideas it's very important to get to the core reason behind their idea.

Is there something you're asking them to do that's making them uncomfortable? Are they being asked to bare their midriff or make out with a Dick Cheney look-alike? (For the record, I have asked actors to do both, and they were completely game.) Rather than say, "I'm uncomfortable breast-feeding a grown man who I just met today," the actor may speak in code and say something like "I don't think my character would do that." Or "I've hurt my back and I'm not coming out of my dressing room." You have to remember that actors are human beings. Which is hard sometimes because they look so much better than human beings. *Is there someone in the room the actor is trying to impress?* This is a big one and should not be overlooked. If a male actor is giving you a hard time about something, you must immediately scan the area for pretty interns.

2) "The show doesn't go on because it's ready; it goes on because it's 11:30."

This is something Lorne has said often about *Saturday Night Live,* but I think it's a great lesson about not being too precious about your writing. You have to try your hardest to be at the top of your game and improve every joke you can until the last possible second, and then you have to *let it go.*

You can't be that kid standing at the top of the waterslide, overthinking it. You have to go down the chute. (And I'm from a generation where a lot of people died on waterslides, so this was an important lesson for me to learn.) You have to let people see what you wrote. It will never be perfect, but perfect is overrated. Perfect is boring on live TV.

What I learned about "bombing" as an improviser at Second City was that bombing is painful, but it doesn't kill you. No matter how badly an improv set goes, you will still be physically alive when it's over. What I learned about bombing as a writer at *Saturday Night* is that you can't be too worried about your "permanent record." Yes, you're going to write some sketches that you love and are proud of forever—your golden nuggets. But you're also going to write some real shit nuggets. And unfortunately, sometimes the shit nuggets will make it onto the air. You can't worry about it. As long as you know the difference, you can go back to panning for gold on Monday.

That's what was so great about Will Ferrell. He would do sketches that were absolutely *his* voice and what (I assume) he loved most—Bill Brasky, Robert Goulet, and

Cowbell—but he would commit just as fully to tap-dancing next to Katie Holmes in the monologue. He's the Michael Caine of sketch comedy. He could be in something awful and it would never stick to him.

3) When hiring, mix Harvard Nerds with Chicago Improvisers and stir.

The writing staff of *Saturday Night Live* has always been a mix of hyperintelligent Harvard Boys* (Jim Downey, Al Franken, Conan O'Brien, Robert Carlock) and gifted, visceral, fun performers (John Belushi, Gilda Radner, Jan Hooks, Horatio Sanz, Bill Murray, Maya Rudolph). Lorne somehow knew that too many of one or the other would knock the show out of balance. To generalize with abandon, if you had nothing but Harvard guys, the whole show would be commercial parodies about people wearing barrels after the 1929 stock market crash. "Flendersen's Poverty Barrels, Replacing Clothes Despite Being More Expensive since… Right Now. Formerly known as Flendersen's Pickles and Suspenders: A Semiotic Exegesis of Jazz Age Excess and the Failings of the Sherman Antitrust Act."

If you had nothing but improvisers, the whole show would be loud drag characters named Vicki and Staci screaming their catchphrase over and over, "YOU KISS YOUR MUTHA WITH THAT FACE?"

---

* I say Harvard "Boys" because they are almost always male—but not exclusively; rock on, Amy Ozols!—and because they are usually under twenty-five and have never done physical labor with their arms or legs. I love them very much.

Harvard Boys and Improv People think differently because their comedy upbringing is so different. If you're at the *Harvard Lampoon,* sitting in a castle with your friends, you can perfect a piece of writing to be exactly what you want and you can avoid the feeling of red-hot flop sweat. Especially because *you won't even be there when someone reads it.* But when you're improvising eight shows a week in front of drunk meat-eating Chicagoans, you will experience highs and lows. You will be heckled, or, worse, you will hear your own heartbeat over the audience's silence. You will be bombing so hard that you will be able to hear a lady in the back put her gum in a napkin. You may have a point to make about the health care system in America, but you'll find out that you need to present that idea through a legally blind bus driver character or as an exotic dancer whose boobs are running for mayor. (I would like to see that sketch, actually.) Ultimately, you will do whatever it takes to win that audience over.

Harvard Is Classical Military Theory, Improv Is Vietnam.

This is all to make the case that Harvard boys and Second City/Groundlings people make beautiful comedy marriages. The Harvard guys keep the Improvisers from wallowing in schmaltz. (Steve Higgins used to joke that every Second City sketch ended with sentimental music and someone saying, "I love you, Dad.")

The Harvard guys check the logic and construction of

every joke, and the Improvisers teach them how to be human. It's Spock and Kirk. (I guess if you want to tie all my metaphors together, it would be Spock wearing a baldric and staying up all night to write a talk show sketch with a mentally ravaged Rambo Kirk.)

I tried to apply Lorne's lesson when staffing *30 Rock*, and it has worked well so far. Our current staff makeup is four Harvard nerds, four Performer-turned-writers, two regular nerds, and two dirtbags.

4) "Television is a visual medium."

Lorne has said this to me a lot. It basically means "Go to bed. You look tired." You may want to be diligent and stay up with the writers all night, but if you're going to be on the show, you can't. Your "street cred" with the staff won't help anybody if you look like a cadaver on camera. Also, don't be afraid to make them get your hair, makeup, and lighting right. It's not vanity, because if you look weird, it will distract from what you're trying to do. If you look as good as you can, people will be able to pay attention to what you're actually saying.

5) "Don't make any big decisions right after the season ends."

This is the same advice they give people who've just come out of rehab. After a grueling period of work (or what passes for grueling work in our soft-handed world) you will crave some kind of reward. Don't let this cause you to rush into a big decision, like a new house or a marriage or partial ownership of a minor league baseball team, that you may later regret. The interesting thing about this piece of advice is that no one ever takes it.

6) "Never cut to a closed door."

Lorne sighed this once in exasperation over some sketch I can't remember. The director had cut to a door a moment too early, before the actor entered, and Lorne felt we "lost the audience" in that moment. This can mean a lot of things: Comedy is about confidence, and the moment an audience senses a slip in confidence, they're nervous for you and they can't laugh. Lorne would have preferred that the camera cut follow the sound of the actor knocking on the door. Which is to say that the sketch should lead the cutting pattern, which is to say content should dictate style, which is to say that in TV the writer is king.

In its most extrapolated version, I think "Never cut to a closed door" means "Don't forget about showmanship." Make the entrance well-timed and exciting. Make the set look pretty at Christmastime. Add some dancers! There's no harm in things looking fun, and you don't get extra credit for keeping things indie and grim.

Or — and this is a distinct possibility — it doesn't mean anything and he was just in a grouchy mood.

7) "Don't hire anyone you wouldn't want to run into in the hallway at three in the morning."

This one is incredibly helpful. We work long hours at

these shows, and no matter how funny someone's writing sample is, if they are too talkative or needy or angry to deal with in the middle of the night by the printer, steer clear. That must be how I got through that first job interview. I was not dynamic, but at least I wasn't nuts.

8) Never tell a crazy person he's crazy.

While never stated overtly, this seems to be Lorne's practice. There were many times in my nine years at the show when I couldn't understand why Lorne wouldn't just tell people to "knock it off." Eccentric writers would turn in sketches that were seventeen minutes long; immature performers tried fits and tears when their sketch was later in the show than they'd like. My every terrible instinct would have been to pull these culprits aside and scold them like a schoolmarm. "Please explain to me why your sketch should get to be three times longer than everyone else's. Why won't you take the perfectly reasonable cuts I suggested?" "How dare you pitch a fit about what time your sketch is on? Some people didn't get to be in the show at all. Do you think you're working harder than everyone else? We're all working hard!" But there is not one management course in the world where they recommend Self-Righteousness as a tool.

Lorne has an indirect and very effective way of dealing with the crazies. It is best described by the old joke that most people know from *Annie Hall*. A man goes to a psychiatrist and says, "My brother's gone crazy. He thinks he's a chicken." And the psychiatrist says, "Have you told him he's not a chicken?" The man replies, "I would, but we need the eggs." Lorne knows that the most exhausting people occasionally turn out the best stuff. How do I explain the presence of crazy people on the staff if we're following Rule #7? Easily: *These* crazy people are charming and brilliant and great fun to see at three in the morning. Also, some people arrive at the show sane and the show turns them crazy.

In fairness to others, I will use myself as an example. In October 2001, Manhattan was a tense place to work. But we all continued to work because it seemed like the Churchillian thing to do. One Friday morning I was sitting in my tiny dressing room at 30 Rockefeller Plaza, trying to write jokes for Weekend Update. I was reading a thick packet of newspaper clippings, looking for something fun to say about Afghanistan, the Taliban, Saddam Hussein, the anthrax postal deaths: It was grim. Then, on the TV hanging in the corner, Lester Holt came on MSNBC and said, "Breaking news. Anthrax has been found at 30 Rockefeller Plaza. CDC officials are investigating the potentially deadly substance, which was found in a suspicious package addressed to *NBC Nightly News* anchor Tom Brokaw and mailed to his offices in 30 Rockefeller Plaza." If you have decent reading comprehension skills you will remember from the beginning of this paragraph that I, too, was at 30 Rockefeller Anthrax Plaza. Not 45 Rockefeller Plaza. Not 1661 Sixth Avenue. 30 Rockefeller Plaza. "Nope," I thought. "I give up." I put on my coat, walked downstairs past my friends and coworkers without saying anything. I walked right past the host for that week, sweet Drew Barrymore, without telling her what I had heard. I just went to the elevator and left. I walked up Sixth Avenue to Central Park West. I walked up Central Park West to 96th Street and across 96th Street to my apartment on West End Avenue, where I would wait to die.

Several hours later, Lorne called and said gently, "We're all here. You and Drew are the only ones who left...and Drew came back a few hours ago, so...We're ordering dinner, if you want to come back in." It was the most gentle, non-Bossypants way of saying "You're embarrassing yourself." I got back to work that evening just in time to find everyone assembled on the studio floor. Andy Lack, the head of NBC News, was addressing the crew in an emergency briefing. Once again, nothing is creepier than a bunch of adults being very quiet. Mr. Lack explained that the envelope was found in the third-floor NBC News offices, so the CDC would be "swabbing" workers from the second floor to the sixth floor, just to be safe. (Remember all those fun catchphrases from 2001? "Swabbing," "Cutaneous," "Cipro," "I am Zoolander.") Some of our camera guys were irate that we on the eighth floor would not be swabbed. They occasionally filled in down in News. The discussion got heated. As I watched from the audience balcony, I remember feeling tremendous affection for everyone there. I felt like we were a family and that if we had to go, at least we'd all go together. I guess I forgot that just a few hours earlier I had booked it out of there, leaving them all to die. I have a uniquely German capacity to vacillate between sentimentality and coldness.

The point is, Lorne did not do what I would have done, which is to say, "You're being crazy. Get back in here. Everyone else is here. Do you think you're more important than everybody else?" He also didn't coddle me, which is what I would have done if I were trying to overcompensate for my natural sternness. "Are you okay? If you need to take a couple days off, I'm sure we can manage, blah, blah, blah."

Instead, he found a way for me to slip back in the door like my mental breakdown never happened. "We're ordering dinner. What do you want?"

He knew how to get the eggs.

Peeing in Jars with Boys

My first show as a writer at *Saturday Night Live* was September 27, 1997. The host was Sylvester Stallone. It was the first time I had ever seen a real movie star up close. Real movie stars do look different from regular people. They are often a little smaller and usually have nicer teeth, shoes, and watches than anyone else in the room. Mr. Stallone smoked a cigar during the host meeting, which was pretty badass. I don't remember what sketch ideas I pitched in that first meeting, but I know that on that first writing night, I completely froze up. I sat at my computer from one P.M. Tuesday afternoon until nine A.M. Wednesday morning and nothing came out. I wasn't used to sitting by myself and writing. I'd been improvising with five other people every night for two years. I ended up submitting an old sketch that I had written as part of my job application.

Needless to say, my sketch didn't get picked for the show, but I was assigned to help "cover" a sketch that

Cheri Oteri had written with another writer. Writers are often assigned to help produce sketches that the performers write. I followed Cheri and writer Scott Wainio around through rehearsal, occasionally pitching jokes for the sketch that were (rightfully) ignored. During the dress rehearsal, Lorne gave us the note that he couldn't understand Stallone in the sketch and we should ask him to enunciate more. I stood nervously outside the host's dressing room with Scott Wainio. He had been there a year already, so I figured he'd know what to do. Scott's experience level was evident when he looked at me and shrugged. "*You* tell him."

My trademark obedience kicked in and I found myself knocking on the door and being ushered in. Judge Dredd himself was on the couch in an undershirt, smoking another cigar. He looked up at me. I muttered, "In the Rita sketch, you were a little hard to understand. Can you just enunciate a little more?" Stallone was unfazed. "Youcannunnastanme? Youneeme nanaunciate maw? Okay." He couldn't have been more easygoing about it. My guess is that this was not the first time in his career he had been given that note. I went back outside and manually released my butt cheeks. Over the years I came to realize that the movie star hosts of the show were just people who wanted to do a good job and (with the exception of a very small handful of d-bags) were eager for any guidance. Who were the d-bags, you ask? I couldn't possibly tell you. But if you want to figure it out, here's a clue: The letters from their names are sprinkled randomly through this chapter.

The only other thing I remember about the Sylvester Stallone show was that they did a Rocky-themed monologue and they needed someone to play Rocky's wife, Adrian. Cheri really wanted the part—she was little, she was from Philly, she could do a good imitation of Talia Shire—but instead, somebody thought it would be funnier to put Chris Kattan in a dress. I remember thinking that was kind of bullshit.

I wasn't privy to the decision-making process at the time; it was my first week, after all. When I reminded producer Steve Higgins of it recently, he (understandably) couldn't remember whose idea it was, and thought that it might have even been Sylvester Stallone's. No offense to Kattan, whom I love, or Sylvester Stallone, but I think Cheri would have been funnier as Adrian. Now, an anecdote about somebody at the show being frustrated and feeling cheated is hardly worth mentioning. It happens to everyone, male or female, at some point every week. *Saturday Night Live* runs on a combustion engine of ambition and disappointment.

But I tell this specific tale of Cheri being passed over for Kattan-in-drag because it illustrates how things were the first week I was there. By the time I left nine years later, that would never have happened. Nobody would have thought for a second that a dude in drag would be funnier than Amy, Maya, or Kristen. The women in the cast took over the show in that decade, and I had the pleasure of being there to witness it.

A FAQ (Freaking Always-asked Question)

People often ask me about the difference between male and female comedians. Do men and women find different things funny? I usually attempt an answer that is so diplomatic and boring that the person will just walk away. Something like "There's a tremendous amount of overlap in what men and women think is funny. And I hate to generalize, but I would say at the far ends of the spectrum, men may prefer visceral, absurd elements like sharks and robots, while women are more drawn to character-based jokes and verbal idiosyncrasies...." Have you walked away yet?

Here's the truth. There is an actual difference between male and female comedy *writers,* and I'm going to reveal it now. The men urinate in cups. And sometimes jars. One of the first times I walked into my old boss Steve Higgins's office, he was eating an apple and smoking a cigarette at the same time. (When I started at *SNL,* you could still smoke in an office building. I might not be young.) I had only been there a few weeks, and Steve had been very encouraging and supportive. I forget what we were talking about, but I went to get a reference book off a high shelf in Steve's office. I reached to move the paper cup that was in front of it, and Higgins jumped up. "Don't touch that. Hang on." He grabbed the cup and a couple others like it around the office and took them out of the room to dump them.

"Oh yeah, that's pee in those cups," my friend Paula later informed me. I could not believe it. I had come from The Second City, which was by no means clean—it would not be unheard-of to see a rat giving birth in an overstuffed ashtray, for example. But I had never heard of anyone peeing in a cup except at a doctor's office. *Maybe* you'd do it on a road trip if it was too far between rest stops. I had definitely never heard of anyone peeing in a cup and leaving it in their own office on a bookshelf to evaporate and be absorbed back into their body through the pores on their face.

I told another male coworker about what I had seen. Was it not the grossest thing he had ever heard? He answered matter-of-factly that he occasionally did it, too. Not all the time. He said it was just something guys did when they were too lazy to go to the bathroom. The bathroom, I should point out, was about as far away as you are from this book. I started to feel like I was from space.

I called Jeff back in Chicago. "You grew up way out in the country with a bunch of brothers. Did you ever pee in cups and, like, leave them around?" Jeff was incredulous. "What? No! That's disgusting." One thousand points for Jeff.

Once I was aware of this practice, I started noticing the cups in other places. In the Weekend Update offices — which were like the smarter-but-meaner older brother of the regular writers' offices — there weren't any cups. There was a jar.* It was a jar of piss with a lid on it, and judging by its consistency, I suspect they sometimes spat into the

---

* When I asked Steve Higgins if he remembered the Weekend Update piss jar he said, "Yes, and be sure you mention the booger that had been wiped on the wall and painted over." So I'm mentioning it.

piss. Or that one of them was terribly ill. You could see it when you came in the door, backlit by the afternoon sun, and at first it seemed to me like a little test. If you saw the piss jar and dared to ignore it and continue into the room, you were welcomed. Welcomed is too strong a word. You were... one of the guys? Nope, you know what? The more I think about it, I'm just projecting. It couldn't have been a test, because they really didn't give a fuck whether you came in the room or not.

And no, *not all of the men whizzed in cups.* But four or five of them out of twenty did, so the men have to own that one. Anytime there's a bad female stand-up somewhere, some dickhead Interblogger will deduce that "women aren't funny." Using that same math, I can state: Male comedy writers piss in cups.

Also, they like to pretend to rape each other. It's... Don't worry about it. It's harmless, actually.

So, to sum up my room-clearing generalizations, men are in comedy to break rules. Conversely, the women I know in comedy are all good daughters, good citizens, mild-mannered college graduates. Maybe we women gravitate toward comedy because it is a socially acceptable way to break rules and a release from our daily life. Have you left me for the cheese tray yet?

Kotex Classic

This is the story of my proudest moment as one of the head writers of *SNL.*

At the beginning of each season, the staff would write commercial parodies—the fake commercials you have enjoyed over the past thirty-five years, such as Schmitt's Gay and Colon Blow. I wish I wrote either of those, but I didn't. (I did write Mom Jeans, Annuale, and Excedrin for Racial Tension Headaches, if that helps.)

Each writer would submit two or three scripts, and the producers and head writers picked which commercials would be shot. We tried to choose carefully because unlike the live sketches, these commercials were shot on film (in the days before HD video) and could cost up to $100,000. It was a big deal to get your commercial parody made because they were permanent. They could repeat forever. Once again, this was in the days before YouTube, so reruns were meaningful, and profitable.

In a normal *SNL* show week, every sketch is read aloud by the cast at a "table read" in front of the whole staff. The room is packed with all the writers, designers, stage managers, musicians, etc., so you have a nice big audience. Everyone can hear where there are laughs and everyone has a sense of which sketches could work. The commercial parodies didn't get that treatment, and choosing which ones to produce always brought out the worst in everyone.

I would read the packet of forty scripts and pick the ones I liked. Dennis McNicholas, the other head writer, would pick the ones he liked. Not surprisingly, we each strongly preferred the ones our friends wrote. (There was an unspoken rule that you *never* pushed for your own piece, ever.)

Then we would each privately corner the producers—Steve Higgins and Tim Herlihy—and try to get them to agree with us. Higgins, Herlihy, Dennis, and I would continue this square dance of selling one another out for a week or so, only to find that Jim Signorelli, the colorful, long-standing director of these taped pieces, had started making whatever parody *he* liked without asking anyone, usually because it had high production values or a visual style he felt like shooting. It's a miracle anything ever got done.

There was one parody script that I really fought for. It was back when "classic" was a big advertising trend. Coke Classic. Reebok Classic. The very very funny Paula Pell had written a script called Kotex Classic. It was as if Kotex were trying to revive nostalgia for those old 1960s maxi pads that hooked to a belt. It featured the women in the cast enjoying fun "modern gal" activities while giant sanitary napkins poked out of their low-rise jeans. It seemed to me like an excellent parody of nostalgia-based marketing while also being a little shocking and silly, which is great for an *SNL* commercial. I kept bringing it up in meetings only to be told that it would be "too difficult to produce." Paula and I weren't sure what that meant, so we kept pressing. Finally, Steve Higgins and Jim Signorelli sat down with us and asked us to explain. "How would we see it? Is it a thing that comes up the front? Would we have to zoom in on it? Wouldn't the girls have to take their pants off? Would we see blood?"

And this was what Oprah would call an Aha Moment

for me. (Trademark Oprah Winfrey; please send a check for eighty-nine cents to Harpo Industries for having read that.) They had never personally experienced the belted maxi pad. It was the moment I realized that there was no "institutionalized sexism" at that place. Sometimes they just literally didn't know what we were talking about. Just as I was not familiar with the completely normal custom of pissing in jars, they had never been handed a fifteen-year-old Kotex product by the school nurse. But they trusted me and Paula, so I'm proud to say we made her commercial and the commercial worked.

Two things were reassuring about this. One, that we were heard. Because Paula was such a goddamn hit factory—she wrote the Cheerleaders, among many other things—they were willing to trust us.

And, more important, for all those years that I was *sure* that boys could tell when I had a loaf-of-bread-size maxi pad going up the back of my pants, they actually had no idea.

I Don't Care If You Like It

(One in a series of love letters to Amy Poehler)

Amy Poehler was new to *SNL* and we were all crowded into the seventeenth-floor writers' room, waiting for the Wednesday read-through to start. There were always a lot of noisy "comedy bits" going on in that room. Amy was in the middle of some such nonsense with Seth Meyers across the table, and she did something vulgar as a joke. I can't remember what it was exactly, except it was dirty and loud and "unladylike."

Jimmy Fallon, who was arguably the star of the show at the time, turned to her and in a faux-squeamish voice said, "Stop that! It's not cute! I don't like it."

Amy dropped what she was doing, went black in the eyes for a second, and wheeled around on him. "I don't fucking care if you like it." Jimmy was visibly startled. Amy went right back to enjoying her ridiculous bit. (I should make it clear that Jimmy and Amy are very good friends and there was never any real beef between them. Insert penis joke here.)

With that exchange, a cosmic shift took place. Amy made it clear that she wasn't there to be cute. She wasn't there to play wives and girlfriends in the boys' scenes. She was there to do what she wanted to do and she did not fucking care if you like it.

I was so happy. Weirdly, I remember thinking, "My friend is here! My friend is here!" Even though things had been going great for me at the show, with Amy there, I felt less alone.

I think of this whenever someone says to me, "Jerry Lewis says women aren't funny," or "Christopher Hitchens says women aren't funny," or "Rick Fenderman says women aren't funny....Do you have anything to say to that?"

Yes. We don't fucking care if you like it.

I don't say it out loud, of course, because Jerry Lewis is a great philanthropist, Hitchens is very sick, and the third guy I made up.

Unless one of these men is my boss, which none of them is, it's irrelevant. My hat goes off to them. It is an impressively arrogant move to conclude that just because *you* don't like something, it is empirically not good. I don't like Chinese food, but I don't write articles trying to prove it doesn't exist.

So my unsolicited advice to women in the workplace is this. When faced with sexism or ageism or lookism or even really aggressive Buddhism, ask yourself the following question: "Is this person in between me and what I want to do?" If the answer is no, ignore it and move on. Your energy is better used doing your work and outpacing people that way. Then, when you're in charge, don't hire the people who were jerky to you.

If the answer is yes, you have a more difficult road ahead of you. I suggest you model your strategy after the old *Sesame Street* film piece "Over! Under! Through!" (If you're under forty you might not remember this film. It taught the concepts of "over," "under," and "through" by filming toddlers crawling around an abandoned construction site. They don't show it anymore because someone has since realized that's nuts.)

If your boss is a jerk, try to find someone above or around your boss who is not a jerk.* If you're lucky, your workplace will have a neutral proving ground—like the rifle range or the car sales total board or the *SNL* read-through. If so, focus on that.

Again, don't waste your energy trying to educate or change opinions. Go "Over! Under! Through!" and opinions will change organically when you're the boss. Or they won't. Who cares?

Do your thing and don't care if they like it.

---

* Is there such a thing as an all-jerk workplace? Yes. I would flat-out avoid working with Wall Street traders or the women who run the changing rooms at Filene's Basement.

Amazing, Gorgeous,
Not Like That

People sometimes ask me, "What's it like to do photo shoots for magazines?" "Do you enjoy that kind of thing?" Let me be completely honest here. Publicity and press junkets are just part of the job. Your work is what you really care about because your work is your craft and your craft is your art and photo shoots are THE FUNNEST!

In case you ever find yourself at a magazine cover shoot (and you might, because Snooki and I have, so anything can happen!), let me tell you what to expect.

It's usually in some cool space called White or Smash House or Jinx Studios. Sometimes it's at an amazing hotel. Wherever it is, it's nicer than where you had your wedding. You take a freight elevator up to a beautiful loft where there is a coffee bar at which everything is free. Free, I say!

I suggest you show up freshly scrubbed with damp hair. Not only is this a courtesy to your hair and makeup team but also it helps to *set the bar low*. Show up looking like an uncooked chicken leg and they can't help but be pleased with the transformation once they get all their makeup on you. I think this is what Jesse Jackson calls the "subtle genius of lowered expectations," but I may be misquoting.

You'll be introduced to the stylist and shown racks and racks of clothes. She has been given your sizes ahead of time and has chosen to ignore them. All the shoes will be too big and all the pants and skirts will be a 5T. The stylists like to figure out a few looks before hair and makeup begins, so you will try on twenty or thirty things. Somebody will put up a makeshift wall by holding a full-length mirror next to an open loft window, and you will strip down naked. You must not look in that mirror at your doughy legs and flat feet, for today is about dreams and illusions, and unfiltered natural daylight is the enemy of dreams.

When you inevitably can't fit into a garment, the stylist's assistant will be sent in to help you. The stylist's assistant will be a chic twenty-year-old Asian girl named Esther or Agnes or Lot's Wife.

In a few years she'll be running the editorial staff, but at this point in time her job is to stuff a middle-aged woman's bare ass crack into a Prada dress and zip it up. In my case, Esther and I are always mutually frustrated when zipping up the tiny dress. Esther is disgusted by my dimply flesh and her low status. I'm annoyed that her tiny hands lack the strength to get Pandora's plague back into the box. "How's it going in there?" calls the stylist passive-aggressively. Reinforcements are called in to push on both sides of my ribcage until the zipper goes up. To avoid conflict, we all blame a third party. "It's these damn invisible zippers!" we say in unison. "I don't know why designers use them!"

The reason none of the dresses fit is because they are "samples." They are from the runway and they were made to fit runway models. Sometimes I can actually fit in the sample size because at five foot four I have the waist size of a seven-foot model. "You can fit in a sample size!" they tell me triumphantly, with the dress straining at the seams, two feet too long on the bottom, and the bra cups hanging right above my navel. They want this to be important to you, so go with it.

Next you are taken to the hair and makeup chair. "Do you have anything on your face?" the makeup artist will ask gently. You don't because, as previously mentioned, you are sandbagging. The makeup artist will then delicately apply expensive moisturizer to your chicken leg while the hair stylist massages your scalp (secretly checking for bald spots).

Once you're moisturized and have enjoyed your free cappuccino, the makeup transformation begins in earnest. They pluck your eyebrows for what seems like twenty minutes even though you have already plucked them fully the night before.

If you're like me, you probably take ten to twelve seconds a day to put on some eyeliner and mascara. Maybe you throw in five seconds of eye shadow if it's New Year's Eve. The makeup artist at your photo shoot will work methodically on your eyelids with a series of tickly little brushes for a hundred minutes. It's soothing, actually, because you must sit still and you absolutely can't do anything else. She will do this thing before she lines your lips where she puts her finger on your top lip and rolls it back ever so gently. When she is done, you look like you have lips! Not crazy overdrawn grandma lips like *you* would do, but God-given lips.

While this is going on, someone gives you a manicure and a pedicure. At really fancy shoots, a celebrity fecalist will study your bowel movements and adjust your humours.

The leg massage and the warm lights of the makeup mirror feel so cozy that you could almost believe that *this* is your actual life instead of that endless degrading "looking for the checkbook" and "boiling macaroni" shit you live with at home.

At some point in the morning, one of the stylists or publicists or fecalists will declare that the free coffee is "not working for me," and some intern is sent out to get other coffee. Or bubble tea. Or gum, Advil, Red Bull, and egg white omelets that are destined to be forgotten about and left on a windowsill.

Only when your makeup is done will they start to do your hair. You hair will be blown straight, then set on large rollers. The hairdresser's assistant hands him rollers and pins on command like an OR nurse. These fashionable young assistants are a fun window into what the rest of us will be wearing three years from now. From what I've seen lately, we can look forward to the return of prairie skirts and the male shag. (The prairie skirts will be on men and the male shag will be on women.)

Once your hair is straightened, it will be curled, then shown to the photographer, who will stare at it with his or her head cocked to one side. Then it will be restraightened.

Depending on the concept for the shoot and the health of your natural hair, you may be asked to wear hair extensions. It's okay. A controlled, photo shoot environment is where extensions belong. Places that are less ideal for hair extensions: the grocery store, women's prison, a water park.

Once your hair and makeup are done, you'll slip into your first look. It will most definitely be one of the dresses that didn't even come close to fitting you, so Lot's Wife will bridge the gap with a thick piece of white elastic and some safety pins. Don't ever feel inadequate when you look at magazines. Just remember that every person you see on a cover has a bra and underwear hanging out a gaping hole in the back. Everyone. Heidi Klum, the Olsen Twins, David Beckham, everybody.

Et voilà! Just two to three hours after your arrival, you are ready to be taken to the photographer and shot.

There are different types of fancy photographers. Some are big, fun personalities like Mario Testino, who once told me, "Lift your chin, darling, you are not eighteen." I enjoyed his honesty. Also, I'm pretty sure he says that to models who are nineteen.

Some photographers plan out every detail of the shot, then plug you into it. For example, with Annie Leibovitz, you might have advance fittings for several custom

Tinkerbell costumes. On the day of the shoot, Annie will pick one of the costumes, then obscure it with a large harness. Afterward, she'll remove the harness with Photoshop, change the color of the costume, and shrink you down to the size of a pea anyway.

There are the nonchalant "cool guy" photographers who shoot for *Rolling Stone* and *GQ*. Watch out for these guys, because their offhand manner can trick you and the next thing you know, you're posing with your pants off. Or worse, with your shoes off.

I'm a firm believer in our constitutional right to wear shoes, and I believe more people should take advantage of it. I never go barefoot during a photo shoot. Even if they say your feet are "out of frame," don't believe them. I know what you're thinking and no, I don't have horrible messed-up feet. Maybe my feet are so amazing that I want to shelter them so they can live a normal life. I don't want them to be the Suri Cruise of feet. Did you ever think about that?

The photographer will ask you what kind of music you want to play during the shoot. Remember that whatever you choose will be blasted through the loft and heard by an entire crew of people who are all so cool that the Board of Ed. officially closed school.

Just murmur, "Hip-hop," or make up the name of a hipster-sounding band and then act superior when they've never heard of it. "Do you guys have any Asphalt of Pinking? [disappointed] Really? [shrug] Whatever *you* want, then."

Sometimes they ask if you want to hook up *your iPod* for background music. Do not do this. It's a trap. They'll put it on shuffle, and no matter how much Beastie Boys or Velvet Underground you have on there, the following four tracks will play in a row: "We'd Like to Thank You Herbert Hoover" from *Annie,* "Hold On" by Wilson Phillips, "That's What Friends Are For," Various Artists, and "We'd Like to Thank You Herbert Hoover" from *Annie.*

To get through the actual shooting process, there are three skills you need to master.

1) Posing

Posing for a successful glamour portrait is very simple. Start with the basics. Turn sideways. Lean back against a wall. Move your chin forward to elongate your neck. Relax your shoulders. Make angles wherever possible. If you're over twenty-four, smile at all times. Keep your arms slightly away from your sides so as not to smush them and make them look larger. Suck your stomach up and in, and wrap your buttocks toward the back, Pilates-style. Be yourself. When you look into the lens, imagine you are looking at a dear friend, but not a friend who would laugh at you for jutting out your chin while arching your back against a fake wall.

Know your weaknesses. For example, I have what can be described as "dead shark eyes." But if I try too hard to look alert, I look batshit crazy, like the runaway bride. If a bout of "creepy face" sets in, the trick is to look away from the camera between shots and turn back only when necessary. This also limits how much of your soul the camera can steal.

2) Dealing with What Is Being Said to You

Most photographers have some kind of verbal patter going on when they shoot: "Great. Turn to me. Big smile. Less shark eyes. Have fun with it. Not like that."

Some photographers are compulsively effusive. "Beautiful. Amazing. Gorgeous! Ugh, so gorgeous!" they yell at shutter speed. If you are anything less than insane, you will realize this is not sincere. It's hard to take because it's more positive feedback than you've received in your entire life thrown at you in fifteen seconds. It would be like going jogging while someone rode next to you in a slow-moving car, yelling, "Yes! You are Carl Lewis! You're breaking a world record right now. Amazing! You are fast. You're going very fast, yes!"

With the wind blowing on your long extensions, you feel like Beyoncé. The moment the wind machine stops, you catch a glimpse of yourself in the mirror and wonder, "Why is the mother from *Coal Miner's Daughter* here?"

Your impulse will be to wilt with embarrassment. Do not! Before you look up for the bucket of pig's blood, remember, your third and most difficult task is "Trying to Enjoy It."

3) Trying to Enjoy It (Proceed as if You Look Awesome)

This requires a level of delusion/egomania usually reserved for popes and drag queens, but you can do it. It's like being a little kid again, parading around in a nightgown tucked into your underpants, believing it looks terrific. Your "right mind" knows that you look ridiculous in a half-open dress and giant shoes, but you must put yourself back in third grade, slipping on your mom's quilted caftan and drinking cream soda out of a champagne glass while watching *The Love Boat*. You have never been more glamorous.

"Believe you are worthy of the cover," as Mario Testino might say to a tense, shark-eyed forty year old.

After about seventeen minutes of shooting, they call lunch. The catered lunch makes you feel like you're finally the person you always wanted to be. Vegetable tartlets. Arugula salad with figs, quinoa, fish that is somehow more flavorful and delicious than a Wendy's hamburger. Miniature lemon meringue pies. Hibiscus iced tea. You fantasize about how wonderful your life would be if you had this food delivered every day. Oh, the energy you would have! Your stools would be museum quality. You could finally impress the fecalist.

At this point someone from your real job or home life will call to check in. Pretend you're exhausted and that this whole photo shoot thing is a big inconvenience. Say you'll be done by six and that you'll be sure to get home in time to help organize the basement storage unit. Then hang up! Do not let those people kill your buzz!

Your afternoon will fly by as you get more and more confident posing like an old Virginia Slims ad.

And then you're done. You get back into this morning's sweatpants, brush out your hair, which by now looks like you've been standing on a tarmac all day, and that's it.

You don't get to keep the clothes, by the way. Some people say that the *really* famous people get to keep the clothes, but I suspect it's just the *pushiest, most deluded* people who get to keep the clothes because they steal them and no one says anything. Your only keepsakes are the individual false eyelashes that you later find stuck to your boob in the shower.

(Someone should do a study of the human brain and how quickly it can adjust to luxury. You could take a homeless person who has been living on the street for twenty years, and if you let them do three magazine photo shoots, by the fourth one they'd be saying, "Louboutins don't really work on me. Can I try the Roger Vivier?" By the fifth one they'd sigh, "Do they not have the vegetable tartlets? Bummer!" in a passive-aggressive tone that means "Somebody go get them.")

You may sink into a slight depression over the next thirty-six hours. You may wonder why your loved ones don't call out, "Amazing, gorgeous, right to me!" as you scramble their eggs.

But just be patient, for in a few weeks, the magazine will be out and you will have incontrovertible proof that you are a young Catherine Deneuve. You casually check the newsstand on your way to buy Bengay heating pads. One day, there it is! Right between Jessica Simpson and those people from *The Bachelor* who murdered each other—it's your face! It *is* your face, right? You can barely recognize yourself with the amount of digital correction. They've taken out your knuckles and given you baby hands. The muscular calves that you're generally very proud of are slimmed to the bone. And what's with the eyes? They always get it wrong under the eyes. In an effort to remove dark circles they take out any depth, and your face looks like it was drawn on a paper plate. You looked forward to them taking out your chicken pox scars and broken blood vessels, but how do you feel when they erase part of you that is perfectly good?

We have now entered the debate over America's most serious and pressing issue: Photoshop.

A lot of women are outraged by the use of Photoshop in magazine photos. I say a lot of women because I have yet to meet one man who could give a fat turd about the topic. Not even a gay man.

I feel about Photoshop the way some people feel about abortion. It is appalling and a tragic reflection on the moral decay of our society...unless *I* need it, in which case, everybody be cool.

Do I think Photoshop is being used excessively? Yes. I saw Madonna's Louis Vuitton ad and honestly, at first glance, I thought it was Gwen Stefani's baby.

Do I worry about overly retouched photos giving women unrealistic expectations and body image issues? I do. I think that we will soon see a rise in anorexia in women over seventy. *Because only people over seventy are fooled by Photoshop.* Only your great-aunt forwards you an image of Sarah Palin holding a rifle and wearing an American-flag bikini and thinks it's real. Only your uncle Vic sends a photo of Barack Obama wearing a hammer and sickle T-shirt and has to have it explained to him that somebody faked that with the computer.

People have learned how to spot it. Just like how everyone learned to spot fake boobs—look for the upper-arm meat. If there's no upper-arm meat, the breasts are fake. Unlike breast implants, which can mess up your health, digital retouching is relatively harmless. As long as we all know it's fake, it's no more dangerous to society than a radio broadcast of *The War of the Worlds*.

Photoshop is just like makeup. When it's done well it looks great, and when it's overdone you look like a crazy asshole. Unfortunately, most people don't do it well. I find, the fancier the fashion magazine is, the worse the Photoshop. It's as if they are already so disgusted that a human has to be in the clothes, they can't stop erasing human features.

"Why can't we accept the human form as it is?" screams no one. I don't know why, but we never have. That's why people wore corsets and neck stretchers and powdered wigs.

If you're going to expend energy being mad about Photoshop, you'll also have to be mad about earrings. No one's ears are that sparkly! They shouldn't have to be! You'll have to get mad about oil paintings—those people didn't really look like that! I for one am furious that people are allowed to turn sideways in photographs! Why can't we accept a woman's full width?! I won't rest until people are only allowed to be photographed facing front under a fluorescent light.

It should absolutely be mandatory for magazines to

credit the person who performed the Photoshop work, just like they do the makeup artist and the stylist...in very tiny white print on white paper.

Some people say it's a feminist issue. I agree, because the best Photoshop job I ever got was for a feminist magazine called *Bust* in 2004.

It was a low-budget shoot in the back of their downtown office. There was no free coffee bar or wind machine, just a bunch of intelligent women with a sense of humor.

I looked at the two paltry lights they had set up and turned to the editors. "We're all feminists here, but you're gonna use Photoshop, right?" "Oh, yeah," they replied instantly. Feminists do the best Photoshop because they leave the meat on your bones. They don't change your size or your skin color. They leave in your disgusting knuckles, but they may take out some armpit stubble. Not because they're denying its existence, but because they understand that it's okay to make a photo look as if you were caught on your best day in the best light.

In an act of amazing bravery, I will let you see this photo of me with Photoshop and without.

There are seven differences. See if you can spot them.*

* Nose thinned. Glasses made less awesome. Grimace inverted. Digital wig swap. Teeth added. Neckline artificially lowered, no cleavage found. Lawn chair removed and sold at yard sale.

Photoshop itself is not evil. Just like Italian salad dressing is not inherently evil, until you rub it all over a desperate young actress and stick her on the cover of *Maxim*, pretending to pull her panties down. (That "thumbs in the panties" move is the worst. Really? It's not enough that they got greased up and in their panties for you, *Maxim*?)

Give it up. Retouching is here to stay. Technology doesn't move backward. No society has ever de-industrialized. Which is why we'll never turn back from Photoshop—and why the economic collapse of China is going to be the death of us all. Never mind that. Let's keep being up in arms about this Photoshop business!

I don't see a future in which we're all anorexic and suicidal. I do see a future in which we all retouch the bejeezus out of our own pictures at home. Family Christmas cards will just be eyes and nostrils in a snowman border.

At least with Photoshop you don't really have to alter your body. It's better than all these disgusting injectibles and implants. Isn't it better to have a computer do it to your picture than to have a doctor do it to your face?

I have thus far refused to get any Botox or plastic surgery. (Although I do wear a clear elastic chin strap that I hook around my ears and pin under my day wig.) I can't be expected to lead the charge on everything. Let me have my Photoshop.

For today is about dreams!

Dear Internet

One of my greatest regrets, other than ~~being the Zodiac Killer~~ never learning to tango, is that I don't always have time to answer the wonderful correspondence I receive. When people care enough to write, the only well-mannered thing to do is to return the gift, so please indulge me as I answer some fans here.

From tmz.com

Posted by Sonya in Tx on 4/7/2010, 4:33 P.M.

"When is Tina going to do something about that hideous scar across her cheek??"

Dear Sonya in Tx,

Greetings, Texan friend! (I'm assuming the "Tx" in your screen name stands for Texas and not some rare chromosomal deficiency you have. Hope I'm right about that!)

First of all, my apologies for the delayed response. I was unaware you had written until I went on tmz.com to watch some of their amazing footage of people in L.A. leaving restaurants and I stumbled upon your question.

I'm sure if you and I compare schedules we could find a time to get together and do something about this scar of mine. But the trickier question is *What* am I going to do? I would love to get your advice, actually. I'm assuming you're a physician, because you seem really knowledgeable about how the human body works. What do *you* think I should do about this hideous scar? I guess I could wear a bag on my head, but do I go with linen like the Elephant Man or a simple brown paper like the Unknown Comic? Too many choices, help!

Thank you for your time. You are a credit to Texas and Viking women both.

Yours,
Tina

P.S. Great use of double question marks, by the way. It makes you seem young.

From Dlisted.com

Posted by Centaurious on Monday, 9/21/2009, 2:08 A.M.

"Tina Fey is an ugly, pear-shaped, bitchy, overrated troll."

Dear Centaurious,

First let me say how inspiring it is that you have learned to use a computer.

I hate for our correspondence to be confrontational, but you have offended me deeply. To say I'm an overrated troll, when you have never even seen me guard a bridge, is patently unfair. I'll leave it for others to say if I'm the best, but I am certainly one of the most dedicated trolls guarding bridges today. I always ask three questions, at least two of which are riddles.

As for "ugly, pear-shaped, and bitchy"? I prefer the terms "offbeat, business class–assed, and exhausted," but I'll take what I can get. There's no such thing as bad press!

Now go to bed, you crazy night owl! You have to be at NASA early in the morning. So they can look for your penis with the Hubble telescope.

Affectionately,
Tina

From PerezHilton.com

Posted by jerkstore on Wednesday, 1/21/2009, 11:21 P.M.

"In my opinion Tina Fey completely ruined SNL. The only reason she's celebrated is because she's a woman and an outspoken liberal. She has not a single funny bone in her body."

Dear jerkstore,

Huzzah for the Truth Teller! Women in this country have been over-celebrated for too long. Just last night there was a story on my local news about a "missing girl," and they must have dedicated seven or eight minutes to "where she was last seen" and "how she might have been abducted by a close family friend," and I thought, "What is this, the News for Chicks?" Then there was some story about Hillary Clinton flying to some country because she's secretary of state. Why do we keep talking about these dumdums? We are a society that constantly celebrates no one but women and it must stop! I want to hear what the men of the world have been up to. What fun new guns have they invented? What are they raping these days? What's Michael Bay's next film going to be?

When I first set out to ruin *SNL*, I didn't think anyone would notice, but I persevered because—like you trying to do a nine-piece jigsaw puzzle—it was a labor of love.

I'm not one to toot my own horn, but I feel safe with you, jerk-store, so I'll say it. Everything you ever hated on *SNL* was by me, and anything you ever liked was by someone else who did it against my will.

Sincerely,
Tina Fey

P.S. You know who *does* have a funny bone in her body? Your mom every night for a dollar.

From a bodybuilding forum

Posted by SmarterChild, on 2/24/2008, 2:10 P.M.

"I'd stick it in her tail pipe."

Dear SmarterChild,

Thank you so much for your interest. Whether you meant it in a sexual way or merely as an act of aggression, I am grateful. As a "woman of a certain age" in this business, I feel incredibly lucky to still be "catching your eye" "with my anus." You keep me relevant!

Sincerely,
Ms. T. Fey

From tmz.com

Posted by Kevin 214 on 11/9/08, 11:38 A.M.

"Tina Fey CHEATED!!!!!! Anyone who has ever seen an old picture of her can see she has had 100% plastic surgery. Her whole face is different. She was ugly then and she is ugly now. She only wished she could ever be as beautiful as Sarah Palin."

Dear Kevin 214,

What can I say? You have an amazing eye. I guess I got caught up in the whole Hollywood thing. I thought I could change a hundred percent of my facial features and as long as I stayed ugly, no one would notice. How foolish I was.

So let's wipe the slate clean. Full disclosure, here is a list of the procedures I've had done. Eye browning, nose lengthening, I get my teeth lightly henna-ed each month to give them their amber luster. I've had my lips thinned, and I've had a treatment called Grimmáge where two fishing wires are run through my jawline and used to gather the skin until it looks like a fancy pillow.

I've had sebaceous implants (small balls of Restylane placed in random locations to give the appearance of youthful neck acne).

I don't have Botox. Unfortunately I'm allergic. Instead I have monthly injections of Bromodialone, a farm-strength rat poison. This keeps my face in a constant state of irritation and paralysis, which of course is indistinguishable from sexual excitement. My face is longer and thinner than it was twenty years ago, and while some might say that is a natural effect of weight loss and aging, you and I know the truth — I pay a woman to sit on the side of my head twice a week. Madonna and Gwyneth go to her, and we've all had amazing results. Ugh, listen to me, I really have changed! Why did I feel the need to name-drop the fact that I'm friends with Madonna Vickerson and Gwyneth Chung?

Since you're so savvy at spotting plastic surgery, I'm sure you've noticed some of my other famous friends who have "had work done." Bishop Desmond Tutu...cheek implants. Supreme Court Judge Ruth Bader Ginsburg? Major tit job. And SpongeBob SquarePants, gender reassignment.

Keep on helpin' me "keep it real,"
T

30 Rock: An Experiment to Confuse Your Grandparents

If you had told me when I was a kid that I would grow up to sit through the annual NBC Employee Sexual Harassment Seminar fourteen times, I would have said, "What's 'sexual harassment'?" because Clarence Thomas didn't invent that until the early nineties. But I would have been very excited to hear that I would spend a large chunk of my adult life working for the Peacock. I love working at NBC. How could I not? I grew up watching *Seinfeld,* Johnny Carson, *Late Night with David Letterman,* and reruns of *The Mothers-in-Law.*

When I was in my eighth season at *Saturday Night Live,* it was time to figure out what the next phase of my life would be. *SNL* is like high school, but at least in high school they tell you when to graduate. It's hard to push yourself out of the nest. Lorne suggested I make a "development deal" with NBC and try to come up with a sitcom. A development deal means they pay you while you're thinking, which is a pretty great deal, unless you're like me and you feel constant anxiety that you haven't thought of anything yet. (My ability to turn good news into anxiety is rivaled only by my ability to turn anxiety into chin acne.) After a few months of getting money for nothing, I pitched NBC president of Primetime Development Kevin Reilly an idea about a cable news producer (me, presumably) who is forced to produce the show of a blowhard right-wing pundit (Alec Baldwin, if we could ever get him) to boost her network's sagging ratings. Kevin Reilly said, "No, thank you." All of a sudden this development deal thing didn't seem so bad. If I could get turned down one or two more times, I could keep the development money but never have to make a show. But then I'd probably also never work again, and I have a very competitive and obedient nature, so...chin acne and rewrites.

Kevin Reilly suggested for my next idea that I write something closer to my life. "Why not write about what it's like to work at *SNL*?" I was reluctant because it seemed self-indulgent to write about the show directly. I had really liked the cable news pitch because I liked the idea of writing Alec Baldwin as a powerful conservative, having him articulate passionately the opposite of everything he believed in real life. My husband, always more clearheaded about these things, suggested that I just keep Alec's character the same. Then I started thinking that if it *was* a show business story, I could use Tracy Morgan, too. A triangle between me, Alec Baldwin, and Tracy Morgan felt like it had potential. These three characters would have completely different views about any topic that came up—

race, gender, politics, workplace ethics, money, sex, women's basketball—and they would agree and disagree in endless combinations.

By 2005 I had fleshed out the idea Kevin Reilly had requested. I would play the head writer of a late-night comedy show. Tracy Morgan would play a lunatic comedy star and Alec Baldwin would play my overbearing conservative boss. Well, it was *written* for Alec Baldwin, but none of us had the balls to talk to him about it yet.

I wrote what they call a "pilot," which means you write the first episode of what you hope will be a long series. Pilot scripts are particularly difficult to write because you have to introduce all the characters without it feeling like a series of introductions. You have to tell a story that's not only funny and compelling but also dramatizes your main characters' points of view and what the series would be about thematically (love, work, investigating sexy child murders in Miami, etc.).

If you want to see a great pilot, watch the first episode of *Cheers*. It's charming, funny, and well constructed. If you want to see an awkward, sweaty pilot episode, watch *30 Rock*. I will not be joining you, because I never want to watch that mess again. (The *30 Rock* writing staff have asked me to stop saying the pilot was terrible, so from here on out I will refer to it as "quirky and unique.")

I met with several excellent actors about playing the role of Jack Donaghy, and with each meeting it became increasingly clear that the part was meant for Alec Baldwin. But I didn't have to work up the nerve to talk to him about it yet, because now I was pregnant and the shooting of the pilot was postponed.

In September, my daughter was born. (For the record: epidural, vaginal delivery, did not poop on the table.) Around Christmastime I was back to work at *SNL*, and Alec was hosting. The show was good that week and Alec was having a good time. Lorne and I looked at each other — should we just ask him?

Lorne asked him and Alec said yes. I stayed out of the room, which is my specialty.

An Auspicious Beginning

NBC executives must have seen something of value in my quirky and unique pilot (Alec Baldwin) because they decided for some reason (Alec Baldwin) to "pick it up." This means they agreed to make eleven more episodes and maybe show them on TV.

The announcement of which shows are picked up each year takes place in May at an advertisers' convention called the "Upfronts." Ad buyers from all kinds of companies gather in New York City for a week. Each day one of the networks presents its "new fall lineup" of shows. They rent out Radio City Music Hall or the Hilton ballroom and try to dazzle the advertisers with exciting clips and personal appearances from their biggest stars. They talk about which "target demographics" they reach and how many "upscale" viewers they have. It is *sexy*, like having-lunch-with-your-parents-after-a-medical-exam sexy.

The advertisers then decide where they want to spend their ad money, and the networks know how much money they'll have to work with in the fall.

We have now exceeded my understanding of the television business.

Right before the 2006 Upfronts, I was called into Lorne Michaels's office at two in the morning after an *SNL* show. "This is it," I thought. "They've come to tell us they want the show." I don't know why I was so confident they would (Alec Baldwin).

I had mixed feelings about this. I now had an eight month old at home, and I wasn't sure that this new seventy-hour-a-week job was, as disgraced politicians say, "in the best interest of my family at this current juncture at the present time."

I was a little excited but mostly blorft. "Blorft" is an adjective I just made up that means "Completely overwhelmed but proceeding as if everything is fine and reacting to the stress with the torpor of a possum." I have been blorft every day for the past seven years.

I went into Lorne's office to receive my good news, but something was up. The CEO of NBC Universal Television Group, Jeff Zucker, was there, and he seemed agitated. Apparently, with all my business savvy, I hadn't realized that Alec Baldwin had not signed up for any episodes beyond the pilot. NBC wanted Alec to sign a new contract before any announcements were made, but Alec, being one of the all-time great Irish ballbusters, would not be rushed.

(Alec and I like to joke now about what I call his "Irish

Negotiating Technique," which usually boils down to his saying: "They offered me more money and I told them to go f*** themselves.")

So Mr. Zucker was being forced to order a show that did not actually have its star in place. He paced around the room. Lorne calmly assured him it would all work out; Alec would eventually sign his contract. Then Lorne waved his hand gently in front of Zucker's face and said, "These are not the droids you're looking for." He didn't, but he might as well have.

"We're really going out on a limb for you here," Jeff Zucker said, wagging his finger at me begrudgingly. "You're picked up." And then, in a most unfortunate Freudian slip, I said, "You're welcome" instead of "Thank you." And that was the glorious becoming of what would go on to be the 102nd most popular show on television.*

Assembling a Team of Ragtag Assassins

Alec did eventually sign his contract, and we started production that August.

My friend and former *SNL* coworker Robert Carlock had moved with his wife and baby from California to New York to be an executive producer and co-head writer on the show. We surrounded ourselves with hardworking, funny people.

---

* Not the 102nd most popular television show of all time. The 102nd most popular television show *of 2006.*

My Bossypants Managerial Techniques

I'll admit that as a female producer I have a tacit "no hot-heads" policy. For years, to be considered a genius at comedy, people had to be "dangerous" and "unpredictable." I have met some very dangerous, erratic, funny people over the years, people I admire, but I don't want to work with them every day. Go do your own show, tough guys, and I will gladly watch it from the safety of my home. I hire the most talented of the people who are the least likely to throw a punch in the workplace. If this is contributing to the Demasculinization of America, I say hold a telethon and let me know how it goes. I don't ever want to get punched in the face over a joke — or even screamed at.

These were those gentle people:

Jack Burditt—a TV veteran who had worked on every show from *Mad About You* to *Frasier* to *DAG*. A handsome, soft-spoken, Gary Cooper type, I don't think Jack said a word the first four weeks. When he finally spoke, it was during a mundane conversation in the writers' room about crappy summer jobs we'd had as teenagers. Jack laughed as he told how at eighteen he was operating the roller-coaster at Magic Mountain and how one night, there was a riot in the park after a disco concert and six people got stabbed. One guy bled out in front of him. Then he turned in a thoughtful and hilarious *30 Rock* script that showed he was more than just a former carnie who had watched a man die. A couple months later he spoke again to tell us how he had once bought a bunch of depth charges and thrown them off the side of a rowboat in Mexico. Also, he believes his torn ACL was healed by a visit to Roswell. And once he fainted in front of Ringo Starr from an undiagnosed testicle infection. Jack's stories were reason enough to keep him around; his elegant scripts were just a bonus. MVP episode: 204, "Rosemary's Baby." MVP joke: this piece of Jack Donaghy wisdom.

<pre>
                    LIZ
          Oh, thank God. It was terrible. I
          went to her apartment. I don't
          think she has a toilet. I saw my
          future, Jack.

Jack pours Liz a drink and hands it to her.

                    JACK
          Never go with a hippie to a second
          location.
</pre>

Kay Cannon was a woman I'd known from the Chicago improv world. A beautiful, strong midwestern gal who had played lots of sports and run track in college, Kay had submitted a good writing sample, but I was more impressed by her athlete's approach to the world. She had a can-do attitude, a willingness to learn through practice, and she was comfortable being coached. Her success at the show is a testament to why all parents should make their daughters pursue team sports instead of pageants. Not that Kay couldn't win a beauty pageant—she could, as long as for the talent competition she could sing a karaoke version of "Redneck Woman" while shooting a Nerf rifle. MVP joke: Tracy Jordan admonishing a pigeon for eating out of the garbage.

```
                    C.C.
                (giving in)
        No one can know we're together,
        Jack. Not even your friend Tracy
        Jordan out there.

                    JACK
        I don't think we have to worry
        about Tracy.

CUT TO: Tracy in front of the building, talk-
ing to a pigeon.

                   TRACY
        Stop eating people's old french
        fries, little pigeon. Have some
        self-respect. Don't you know you
        can fly?
```

Dave Finkel and Brett Baer were a writing team from LA, and I'm proud to say that during that first year they contributed some of our weirdest material. MVP episode: 118, "Fireworks," in which Tracy finds out he is a descendant of Thomas Jefferson. MVP scene: Tracy, anxious over this change in his racial identity, dreams that he is on a paternity test episode of *The Maury Povich Show* with

Thomas Jefferson. Played, for dream-logic and financial reasons, by Alec Baldwin.

> MAURY POVICH
> Sally Hemings just called you a dog,
> Thomas Jefferson.

> THOMAS JEFFERSON
> I don't care. This is about Tracy.
> I rode a horse all the way from
> Heaven to tell him something.

There was Matt Hubbard, a baby-faced Harvard boy who always wanted to order McDonald's for staff lunch, which I liked a lot. Matt and his wife sublet a place on the Upper East Side of Manhattan that turned out to have bedbugs.

This kind of deep human suffering, in combination with his highly processed diet, transformed him into a joke-writing superhero. MVP episode: 115, "Hardball." MVP joke: Tracy Jordan on food.

```
                    KENNETH
          Hello there, Mr. Jordan! Mr. Slattery,
          Mr. Oppenheim. I've picked up your lunch
          from Sylvia's. Extra cornbread, because
          I know you like it.

                    TRACY
          Like it? I love it! I love that corn-
          bread so much I want to take it out
          behind the middle school and get it
          pregnant!
```

There was Daisy Gardner, a delicate soul with a nervous stomach who pitched some of the filthiest jokes you could imagine, in the gentlest voice you could imagine. MVP episode: 116, "The Source Awards," in which Jack Donaghy tries to recover from the failure of his foul-tasting wine, Donaghy Estates, by trying to market it to the hip-hop community as a replacement for Cristal. MVP joke: rapper Ghostface Killah trying to swig Donaghy Estates during a music video.

```
               GHOSTFACE KILLAH (CONT'D)
          'CAUSE I GET RAW AND TAKE
          NAMES/JUST LIKE LEBRON JAMES/AND
          DONAGHY KINDA RHYMES WITH
          PARTY/WHICH IS COOL —
```

He takes another sip, reacts, disgusted.

> GHOSTFACE KILLAH (CONT'D)
> I gotta take a break. I can't drink any
> more of this. My tummy hurts!

The Lord sent me John Riggi, who upon first meeting looked like an angry longshoreman in a denim jacket and a skullcap, but turned out to be a sensitive Italian boy from Cincinnati and an excellent cook. MVP episode: 104, "Blind Date." MVP joke:

> LIZ
> You mean Gretchen Thomas? The brilliant
> plastics engineer-slash-lesbian?
>   (off his puzzled look)
> What made you think I was gay?

> JACK
> Your shoes.

Liz looks down at her shoes. They are pretty borderline.

> LIZ
> Well, I'm straight.

> JACK
> Those shoes are bi-curious.

Our youngest writer was Donald Glover. He had just graduated from NYU's writing program and was still living in a dorm and working as an RA. Donald was our only African American writer at the time, but his real diversity was that he was our only "cool young person" who could tell us what the "kids were listening to these days." Also, because he came from a large family in Georgia, he was very helpful in writing for the character Kenneth the Page. MVP joke: a scene where Jenna (Jane Krakowski) is trying to teach Kenneth (Jack McBrayer) how to brag about himself in a passive-aggressive way.

```
                  JENNA
   Not even a "back door" brag?

                 KENNETH
   What's a "back door" brag?

                  JENNA
   It's sneaking something wonderful about
   yourself into everyday conversation.
   Like when I tell people, "It's hard for
   me to watch 'American Idol,' because I
   have perfect pitch."

                 KENNETH
   Oh...ew.

                  JENNA
   Now you try.

                 KENNETH
   It's hard for me to watch "American
   Idol" 'cause there's a water bug on
   my channel changer.
```

182 · Tina Fey

It's hard for me to pinpoint what I like most about that joke. Is it that Kenneth is truly incapable of bragging? The revelation that Kenneth's apartment is crawling with water bugs? No, I think it's the use of the grandmotherly expression "channel changer."

As for Robert Carlock, his strengths are erudite references, absurd joke constructions, and White Male Malaise in a multicultural world. MVP episodes: 107, "Jack-tor"; 214, "Sandwich Day"; 310, "Generalissimo"; 316, "Apollo, Apollo." MVP joke: too many to name, but the character that flows from him the most freely is Dr. Leo Spaceman (Chris Parnell). At the end of season 1, Jack suffers a heart attack. His unscrupulous showbiz doctor comes out to the waiting room to give Liz, Jack's mother (Elaine Stritch), and Jack's fiancée (Emily Mortimer) a prognosis.

Dr. Spaceman enters from I.C.U. His lab coat is covered in blood. The women all gasp.

> DR. SPACEMAN
> What, this? No, no, I was at a costume
> party earlier this evening...and the
> hostess's dog attacked me so I had to
> stab it.

Perhaps the Carlockian worldview is best summed up by this exchange from a recent episode, when Tracy arrives at the hospital just after the birth of his daughter.

TRACY (O.C.) (CONT'D)
Why is the baby covered in goop?!

DR. SPACEMAN (O.C.)
Because everything about this is
disgusting!

Taking the World by Storm!
(Storm Downgraded to Light Rain by
Weather Experts)

We premiered on Wednesday, October 11, 2006, at 8:00 P.M. and we were an instant hit — like figs for dessert or bringing your guitar out at a party. We were New Coke!

We were not a hit.

But we barreled ahead knowing that we'd at least come out of this with DVDs to show our friends. The story ideas came fast and furious in the beginning. "What if Tracy went off his medication and started hallucinating a little blue dude everywhere?" Sure. "What if Jenna was in a movie called *The Rural Juror* and no one could understand her when she said the title?" Fine. "What if we do a story about Liz being called a cunt?" Why wouldn't we? That had happened to me plenty!*

You know that saying "Dance as if no one is watching"?

---

* Actually, that only happened to me once that I know about. A coworker at *SNL* dropped an angry C-bomb on me and I had the weirdest reaction. To my surprise, I blurted, "No. You don't get to call me that. My parents love me; I'm not some Adult Child of an Alcoholic that's going to take that shit." And it never happened again...that I know of.

Well, that's what we were doing. We were dancing with abandon, and no one was watching. Actually, about five and a half million people were watching, but that counts as nothing. In my Chicago theater days, the rule was there had to be more people in the audience than on the stage or we cancelled the show. Although once I did a two-woman play called *Ironmistress* for an audience of two. So five million people seemed pretty good to me. But back when *Friends* was in its prime, they had about twenty-five million viewers. We were in jeopardy.

I don't think Robert Carlock unpacked his suitcase that whole first year. He probably didn't even buy full gallons of milk, assuming we'd be cancelled any minute and he'd have to chug the whole thing and get back on the plane to Los Angeles.

I proceeded with the blithe confidence of a moron. I was the baby in the movie *Baby's Day Out,* toddling down the street, completely unaware that an anvil had just fallen behind me.* Conversely, every time the office phone rang, Robert put his coat on. That was the burden of his higher intelligence.

We worked incredibly hard that first year, and every year since. Carlock and I can't believe we used to complain about the hours at *SNL,* which now seem like a cakewalk. Especially for me, because that's all I did my first two years at *SNL:* walk around and look for cake. For context,

---

* Although good news gives me angina, I am impervious to bad news. I should be in one of those Oliver Sacks books, because surely I have a rare head injury.

I've attached a chart that shows the relative stress levels of various jobs.

Jeff Zucker and NBC president of Primetime Development Kevin Reilly proved to be real champions of the show. We started making jokes about NBC and its then parent company, GE, almost immediately. We didn't have anything against GE or even really know anything about GE, but we had painted ourselves into a corner by making it Jack Donaghy's workplace in the show. When Carlock got a call one day from a woman in the GE Legal Department disputing the accuracy of a GE mention in one of our scripts, we were confused and nervous. Why does the parent company have our scripts? Is this going to happen every week? Don't they know I'm the baby from *Baby's Day Out*? Apparently it was Mr. Zucker who personally intervened and explained to his more corporate peers that these were just jokes and we were to be left alone. Maybe he assumed we'd be dead soon. Whatever the reason, I appreciate NBC for letting us make jokes about them all the time. I don't think ABC or CBS would stand for that abuse, and I'll probably never find out.

Doing, Learning, Dying

We shoot *30 Rock* on film, like a little movie each week. This means that we film every line of dialogue about five times from about five different angles. Every time we switch angles it takes about twenty minutes to move the cameras around. Every five minutes the cameras run out of

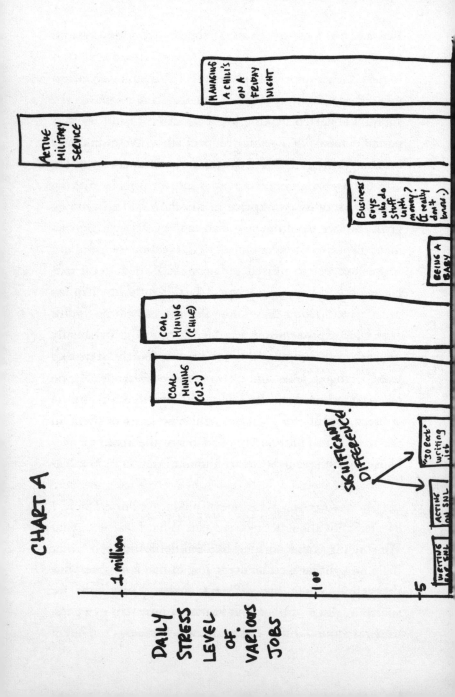

film and we have to reload. If someone's getting on our fake elevator in a scene, it usually takes an extra five tries to have the elevator door close at the right time. You don't even want to know what happens if there's a dog, cat, parrot, baby, or peacock in the shot. And worst of all, our cast and crew like one another and enjoy lively conversations. All this jocularity adds up to about fourteen hours a day.

(If we shot on this newfangled hi-def video it would go faster, but we would look like the zombie backup dancers in *Thriller*.)

We only shoot in this "single camera" style because it is currently the fashion. Classic shows like *Frasier, Everybody Loves Raymond,* and *Seinfeld* were shot "multicamera" in front of an audience. I'm pretty sure it took about three hours a week. I don't know why the network's taste changed to single-camera shows, but there's no bucking fashion trends. If that were possible, I'd still be wearing this amazing pair of light blue jeans I owned in college that had four built-in belts across the front.

That first season when we shot on location in Manhattan, people would stop to watch before realizing we were not *Sex and the City,* when they would leave immediately. I learned a lot about acting that year. What I learned about Film Acting is that it's mostly about not standing in other people's light, and remembering what hand you had your papers in. When you do your "off-camera" lines for someone, you try to put your head real close to the camera. That's about it. You're a trained film actor now.

Anything I learned about Real Acting I learned from watching Alec Baldwin. By Real Acting I mean "an imitation of human behavior that is both emotionally natural and mechanically precise enough as to elicit tears or laughter from humans." Alec is a master of both Film Acting and Real Acting. He can play the emotion at the core of a scene—he is falling in love, his mother is torturing him, his mentor has been reincarnated as a peacock—while reciting long speeches word for word and hitting all the jokes with the right rhythm. You would be surprised how many major Oscar-winning movie stars cannot do this. There are only about nine people in the world who can do this; maybe three more that we don't know about in North Korea.

Alec knows how to let the camera come to him. He can convey a lot with a small movement of his eyes. He speaks so quietly sometimes that I can barely hear him when I'm standing next to him, but when you watch the film back, it's all there.

It may not have made me a better actor, but at least now I know why what I'm doing is terrible.

After each fourteen-hour acting class was over, I would meet up with five or six writers at my apartment to catch up on what they had written during the day. During those early days we'd order food and work until one or two in the morning. My husband, Jeff, sat in what was meant to be a pantry and wrote music to score the show. We kept a video baby monitor next to the computer screen, and I could watch my daughter sleeping while we worked. I would excuse myself occasionally to change a diaper in the night. Usually for the baby. These will definitely be my happiest memories of this time, because everything I cared about was within ten feet of me. One night I put my daughter to bed, worked with the writers all night, and in the morning when she toddled out, the writers were still there. It was the best worst thing ever.

Another night to remember: Around three A.M., Carlock and I were leading a rewrite in my living room and realized that we had both fallen asleep while talking. When we woke up a few moments (or hours?) later, the other writers were just sitting politely, awaiting further instruction. That is a dedicated staff.

The only downside was that the next day's work began at six A.M. In spite of the exhaustion, I am proud to say I lost my cool only once, in my kitchen. "It's too much. It's just too much work," I sobbed to my husband. Please refer to the Coal Mining and Military Service sections of Chart A for perspective.

I turned to domestic violence only once. We were going to bed at three A.M., knowing we'd have to get back up at five thirty A.M., and my husband kept talking and talking as a joke when I was trying to fall asleep. His exhaustion had given him the giggles, and he kept poking me and waking me up saying things like "Hey, I gotta ask you one more thing. Do you like pretzels?" I flew off my pillow and shoved him so hard across the bed that I saw genuine fear flash across his face. It was one of the very few "deleted scenes from *Star 80*" in my life.

There is one other embarrassing secret I must reveal, something I've never admitted to anyone. Though we are grateful for the affection *30 Rock* has received from critics and hipsters, we were actually trying to make a hit show. We weren't trying to make a low-rated critical darling that snarled in the face of conventionality. We were trying to make *Home Improvement* and we did it wrong. You know those scientists who were developing a blood-pressure medicine and they accidentally invented Viagra? We were trying to make Viagra and we ended up with blood-pressure medicine.

No matter how many times we tried to course-correct the show to make it more accessible — slow the dialogue down, tell fewer stories per episode, stop putting people in blackface — the show would end up careening off the rails again. In my limited experience, shows are like children. You can teach them manners and dress them in little sailor suits, but in the end, they're going to be who they're going to be.

By episode eleven *30 Rock* had really found its voice, and it was the voice of a crazy person. The episode ended up being called "Black Tie," but while we were shooting we referred to it as "Good-bye, America." We were coming to the end of our initial order and there was no sign of our being picked up again. The other reason we were calling it "Good-bye, America" was because this episode was nuts. If we had any concern that the show was too weird to suc-ceed, we certainly weren't helping ourselves with this one. The main story of the episode is that Alec's character, Jack

Donaghy, attends a birthday party for his friend, an inbred Austrian prince named Gerhardt Hapsburg.

Gerhardt Hapsburg was played by Paul Reubens, the genius known to most as Pee-wee Herman. Paul committed deeply to his role. He chose to wear fake teeth and pale makeup, and he had one tiny ivory hand (years before Kristen Wiig's tiny hands on *SNL*, our writers would want me to point out). In case you were wondering if *30 Rock* would ever be a commercial hit, look at this picture.

In the story, Jenna (Jane Krakowski) is determined to "Grace Kelly" herself by meeting and marrying Gerhardt and becoming a princess. This culminates in a scene where she dances for the prince. Jane danced (like no one was watching) as Paul improvised, calling out different dance styles: "Jazz! Tap! Jitterbug! Charleston! Interpretive! Twirl! Twirl again! Keep twirling!" After he professes his love for Jenna and she reciprocates, Gerhardt takes a sip of celebratory champagne, knowing that it will kill him because his malformed body cannot metabolize grapes. He dies immediately. This was our best attempt at writing a sitcom.

Poor Gerhardt serves as a metaphor for the show itself—strange but not stupid, desperate to be loved but abhorrent to most. A proud member of an aristocracy that no longer existed—network television.

Some Unsolicited Theories About Television

Gerhardt's picture leads me to something else I'd like to acknowledge, which is what a human-looking cast we are. Sure, Alec has a movie star face and Jane is leggy and blond, but the cumulative age of our series regulars is 210, and even the African Americans among us are pretty pasty. I personally *like* a cast with a lot of different-shaped faces and weird little bodies and a diverse array of weak chins, because it helps me tell the characters apart. When actors are too good-looking, I can't memorize them. For example, I have never seen a picture of Sienna Miller where I didn't say, "That girl's pretty. Who is that?"

For years the networks have tried to re-create the success of *Friends* by making pilot after pilot about beautiful twenty-somethings living together in New York. Beautiful twenty-somethings living in Los Angeles. Beautiful twenty-somethings investigating sexy child murders in Miami.

This template never works, because executives refuse to realize that *Friends* was the exception, *not the rule*. The stars of beloved shows like *Cheers, Frasier, Seinfeld, Newhart,* and *The Dick Van Dyke Show* had normal human faces. And that's what some of the people on our show have.

When you watched *Sanford and Son*, you didn't want to have sex with everybody you saw, just Grady. I've never understood why every character being "hot" was necessary for enjoying a TV show. It's the same reason I don't get Hooters. Why do we need to enjoy chicken wings and boobies at the same time? Yes, they are a natural and beautiful part of the human experience. And so are boobies. But why at the same time? Going to the bathroom is part of life, but we wouldn't go to a restaurant that had toilets for seats... or *would we?* Excuse me while I call my business manager.

He said it's a "nonstarter." They already have that in Japan.

The week after "Good-bye America," we shot episode twelve, which was called "The Baby Show." It was officially the last show of our order. Members of our crew were calling around looking for their next job. On set, people started eyeing the furniture, wondering what it would go for in the Cancellation Fire Sale.

Don Fey happened to be visiting the set that last week when Kevin Reilly called to say that we were picked up for the rest of the season. I may never know why they chose to keep the show going (Alec Baldwin), but my proudest moment as an adult was walking back onto the soundstage and telling everyone they still had jobs. (My proudest moment as a child was the time I beat my uncle Pierre at Scrabble with the seven-letter word FARTING.)

By March, the first season of *30 Rock* was complete. (For the record: no epidural, group vaginal delivery, did not poop on the table.) That September we won the Emmy for Outstanding Comedy Series.

Now, I know I'm not saying anything that hasn't been said hundreds of times, but *30 Rock* is the perfect symbol for the pro-life movement in America. Here's this little show that no one thought would make it. I'm sure NBC considered getting rid of it, but by the time we won the Emmy, they were too far along.

As the mother of this now five-year-old show, would I still rather have a big, strong *Two and a Half Men* than our sickly little program? No, I would not, because I love my weird little show. I think this show was put on earth to teach me patience and compassion.

"The Days Are Long and the Years Are Short" —Stay-at-Home Moms and Sex Workers

Now that we've finished season 5, it's time to start shopping for parachutes again. Rob Reiner was a guest on the show this year, and he went out of his way to tell us all to appreciate this job. Jobs like this are special and they don't last forever. No need to remind me, Michael Stivic. I have seen my future, and it is a weight-loss game show on Lifetime. And I don't even win.

Here are answers to some FAQ about 30 Rock:

Q: Is Alec Baldwin really leaving show business?

A: I don't know, but we do have a contingency plan: a slightly out of focus Billy Baldwin.

Q: Is Tracy Morgan as wild and crazy as his character?

A: There's only one way for you to find out. Drive across country with him in a Prius.

Q: Will Jack and Liz ever "hook up"?

A: In spite of their "Sam and Diane" sparring, their relationship will remain more like "Norm and Cliff" — making out while drunk and then denying it.

Q: When is it on, again?

A: Thursdays at either 10:00 or 8:30 or … you know what? Just DVR it.

Q: Where did you find Grizz and Dotcom?

A: Grizz and Dotcom were born adorable and fully clothed and found nestled in a field. They were the inspiration for the Cabbage Patch dolls and the Cabbage Patch dance.

Q: When are we gonna see more of Pete and the writers?

A: Season 9.

Q: Has Tracy Morgan ever French-kissed an NBC executive?

A: Yes, but only at an official NBC event, and only against her will.

Q: Is Jack McBrayer really like his character?

A: No, Jack's character is a simple farm boy from Stone Mountain, Georgia. Jack himself would be useless on a farm, and he's from the bank-robbery and teen-sex-scandal metropolis of Conyers, Georgia.

Q: How come Liz Lemon talks so much about food and overeating but she's not fat?

A: The character Liz Lemon has a rare condition called "orophasmia," where everything she eats immediately falls out her bottom like a ghost. This was established in episode 219, "The One About Liz's Orophasmia," in the roller-coaster scene with Emmy-nominated guest star Marisa Tomei.

Q: Is *30 Rock* the most racist show on television?

A: No, in my opinion it's NFL football. Why do they portray all those guys as murderers and rapists?

Q: How many janitors work at *TGS*, the fictional show within the show?

A: We have established eight distinct janitorial characters. Joe, Subhas, Old Janitor, Rolly, Khonani, Euzebia, Rosa, and Jadwiga.* Action figures are in the works.

---

* I am proud to say that since the hardcover edition of this book was printed, we have added another janitor, Tom, as played by the great Michael Keaton.

Sarah, Oprah, and Captain Hook, or How to Succeed by Sort of Looking Like Someone

I would never have made it into the cast of *Saturday Night Live* if I'd had to go about it in the regular way. When people audition for the show, they have to stand on the historic *SNL* home base stage and try to get a laugh from the four or five stone-cold strangers watching them. They have to demonstrate their funny characters and voices, of which I have none. My own child could tell you that my "funny voices" are completely derivative and my Mr. Smee impression sounds nothing like the guy in the movie.

I ended up on TV because Lorne Michaels likes to promote from within. When he had to choose who would replace David Letterman in *Late Night* on NBC, he picked unknown former *SNL* writer Conan O'Brien. When it was time to pick new anchors for Weekend Update in 1999, he did a nationwide talent search that went all the way across the hall. He let one of the head writers of the show — me — do a screen test with cast member Jimmy Fallon. By the time I tested for the show, I had already worked there for three years. I wasn't intimidated by anyone in the room, and I already had a day job *at the show* to fall back on. I didn't have to do characters, just read jokes without messing up.

The timing of the Weekend Update turnover was, at that point in my life, the luckiest, craziest thing that had ever happened to me.

In rehearsing for the screen test, I realized that I couldn't see the cue cards. I've worn glasses to see far away since I was twenty-one, but I only need them for a few activities, like going to the movies, finding Orion's belt, and reading cue cards. So I went to the doctor and got my first pair of contact lenses. The day of the screen test I spent about twenty-five minutes nervously trying to get the lenses onto my eyeballs. Right up until camera time, I was sweaty and green from having to touch my own eyeballs like that. If you've never had to do it, I'd say it's not quite as quease-making as when you lose your tampon string, but equally queasish to a self–breast exam. If you are male, I would liken it to touching your own eyeball, and thank you for buying this book.

Jimmy and I did a screen test, as did a bunch of other people in the cast and several comics from the outside world. Because Jimmy was a star and Lorne felt that I would make sure the writing of the segment got done, Jimmy and I got the job.

We did another camera test for set and lighting. Less than eager to touch my own eyeballs again, I just wore my glasses the second time around. After the test, the great comedy writer and chronicler of human perversions T. Sean

Shannon came up to me and said in his Texas drawl, "You should leave them glasses on, sister." And so, a commonplace librarian fetish was embraced for profit.

Once I was hired to do Update, every now and then the writers would put me in a sketch. This usually happened only if all the other women were already in the sketch and they had run out of bodies. But they didn't use me much, because I could never really look like anybody else. Molly Shannon has a great face for wigs. Her features are delicate and symmetrical, and her coloring is neutral enough that she can play a blond Courtney Love or raven-haired Monica Lewinsky and you buy it. Maya Rudolph's face can change from Donatella Versace to Beyoncé in a minute and seventeen seconds. I always just look like me, in a wig. (See below pictures of me not resembling Dina Lohan, Janice Dickinson, or Barbara Pierce Bush.)

The closest I ever came to looking like anyone else was when they tried to dress me up like a bearded lady from the circus and I looked just like my brother. It has something to do with the fact that my eyes and eyebrows are very dark but my skin is very pale and my nose is kind of long. I was absolutely useless when it came to being a look-alike.

So You Can Imagine My Surprise...

So you can imagine my surprise on August 29, 2008, when my husband called me into the room to watch CNN. John McCain had selected first-term Alaska governor Sarah Palin as his running mate, and two things were obvious right away. One, this was a craven attempt to lure Hillary voters away from Obama, and two—"She kind of looks like you," my husband said. I scoffed. It was just that she had brown hair and glasses. But the e-mails started coming, from friends and cousins and coworkers. People seemed to think we really looked alike. The most powerful minds in the world—cable news anchors and Internet users—started speculating as to whether I would play her on *Saturday Night Live*.

We had already done two full seasons of *30 Rock* and were just beginning to shoot season 3. If I had been wondering whether people were aware of the new show, the answer was now clear; *they were not*. No one had even noticed that I didn't work at *Saturday Night* anymore. Also, no one seemed to remember that when I *did* work there, I only did the news. They didn't care. They were in a blind frenzy. "Brown hair! Glasses!"

In a Shocking Turn of Events...

In a shocking turn of events, Oprah Winfrey had expressed the slightest polite interest in being on *30 Rock*. Desperate to find a larger audience, we jumped at this chance like meth heads over a cough syrup counter. Robert Carlock wrote a hilarious script where Liz Lemon meets Oprah on a plane. (You can buy it on iTunes!) We sent the script to some women at Harpo, who told us that Oprah liked it and they were sure she would do it. We were ecstatic. As the summer wore on, however, it became clear that Oprah had not actually seen the script. In late August, Oprah's chief of staff (I am not joking) called to say that Oprah was really sorry but she would not be able to do the show. This was planned as our second episode of the season, and Oprah was irreplaceable in it. We had already shot half the episode. If this fell apart now, it would cost the show hundreds of thousands of dollars. I had the nerve-racking task of getting on the phone with Ms. Winfrey and trying to talk her into it. I am terribly, terribly suited for such jobs. I'm shy and have no salesmanship — I am actually able to convey sweaty palms over the phone. I didn't try to sell Ms. Winfrey on the comedy of the episode; instead I appealed to her knowledge of television schedules and how royally cornholed we'd be if she declined. She listened, because she is smart and generous. She agreed to let us do a rewrite of the script and consider it, but I knew that until that Oprah footage was "in the can," I would carry around a very specific form of physical anxiety that feels kind of like my heart shrinking up like a raisin.

Meanwhile, Across Town...

Meanwhile, across town, the staff of *Saturday Night Live* was preparing to start their season early, on September 13, to cover this very important national election. The show is always exciting during election years and has proven its

202 · Tina Fey

political relevance time and time again over its thirty-five-year run. (I have to include sentences like that because I'm trying to get college credit for this.)

On September 3, 2008, then governor Palin accepted the vice presidential nomination. Around this same time, Oprah formally agreed to be on *30 Rock,* and it was determined that my daughter's third-birthday party would have a Peter Pan theme. Each of these events was equally important in my life.

Lorne and I discussed the overwhelming public opinion (hyperbole) that I should play Governor Palin. Apparently, that morning both Lorne's doorman and Robert De Niro had stopped him to say how uncanny the resemblance was. Did we dare disappoint Frank the Doorman and Robert De Niro?

Lorne and I shared the same hesitation: If everyone in the world had the same casting idea, it couldn't possibly be a *good* idea, right? When you work at *SNL,* people come up to you all the time and say stuff like "You know what you should do? A skit about my brother-in-law," or "You should do a skit where Tiger Woods and Obama are gay for each other." Or "That show hasn't been good since the seventies." People always have lots of opinions about the show and they're never right, so why would they be right now?

But Lorne is also an old-school producer, and somewhere deep down I think he knew that if he cast me in the part "by popular demand," even if I sucked, it might be a good rating. A good rating is a good rating, even if people tune in just to be mad about how much it sucked.

We decided not to decide. This is another technique I'd learned from Lorne. Sometimes if you have a difficult decision to make, just stall until the answer presents itself.

Back at 30 Rock...

Back at *30 Rock* we scheduled our shooting day with Miss Oprah Winfrey. She generously offered to fly in on Saturday, September 13, to pick up her scenes. This was perfect. I could safely plan my daughter's party for Sunday the 14th. The only remaining problem was that I could not find Peter Pan plates or cups. You can find Tinkerbell or Captain Hook, but no Peter Pan. Was Disney in some kind of legal conflict with the J. M. Barrie estate? There was no time to get involved in that! I had less than a week! Captain Hook cups mixed with Tinkerbell plates would have to suffice.

It was four days until the season premiere of *SNL* and still no decision from Lorne. I was walking around the *30 Rock* offices telling everyone that I couldn't possibly play Palin—I was too busy and I didn't do impressions and it's important to say no sometimes and I couldn't possibly commit to it—but in the back of my head, I was very aware that no one had actually asked me to do it. "Has he called you yet? Has he called you yet?" my friends were asking. Nope. I slumped against my locker and twirled my ponytail.

I had arrogantly thought it was all about me and whether I felt like doing it, but of course it was *Lorne's* decision to make and not mine. It's *his* show.

Still trying to control the situation, I called Lorne's

204 • Tina Fey

office on Wednesday evening after their read-through and
left a message to say I didn't want to play Palin, should it
come up. My call was not returned.

On Wednesday night, Alice and I drew a picture of
Peter Pan to hang up at the party. I explained to her the
apparent licensing problem with the plates. She was
understanding and suggested we relax by pretending to be
Wendy and a mermaid for the next sixty-five minutes.

On Thursday, Oprah's office checked in to say that
she had heard I might be doing *Saturday Night Live* that
Saturday and would I rather reschedule her shoot? No,
no, no! Get the "O" in the can, for the sake of my heart
raisin.

Thursday morning I checked the status of my Amazon
.com order. The birthday present I had ordered was not
here yet. I also started peeking at YouTube clips of Sarah
Palin. How hard could that voice be?

On Thursday evening, Lorne called to say that Seth
Meyers had written a piece and I should come over late
Friday evening and rehearse it with Amy and if it didn't
feel right, someone else would do it.

I rambled through my concerns. Kristen Wiig would
be better at it. (Lorne agreed.) I felt that whatever I appeared
in, people would assume that I wrote it and that it was
expressing my personal opinions. These were delusions of
grandeur, of course; remember, no one even noticed that I
had quit. Regardless, I didn't want to be a stock character
that any writer on the staff could make use of. I didn't
want, for example, to play Sarah Palin in a sketch about
how Hillary Clinton was a jealous dyke or something.

Also, I was skittish to do political comedy after getting myself into trouble a few months before.

My Mouth Goes into Politics.
The Rest of Me Is Forced to Follow.

After the Writers Guild of America Strike that Changed the World in 2008, I was asked to host the first Saturday Night Live back on the air. Finally, the world would see my full range of comedy characters—from grouchy librarian to Russian librarian.

Seth and Amy asked if I wanted to come on Weekend Update to do a "Woman News" segment. The piece the Update writers and I threw together was meant to be about the way Hillary Clinton was being treated and perceived during the campaign. It was meant to point out that America seemed more comfortable with a male minority candidate than a white female candidate. It was meant to discuss (in joke form) that people didn't take to Hillary because of this vague feeling that she was kind of a bitch and how unfair that was. It was meant to be about gender politics, not actual politics.

What came out was an overt Hillary Clinton endorsement.

It wasn't that I didn't like Mrs. Clinton as a candidate; it's just that Weekend Update features are written so hastily. If you're hosting, you don't even start writing them until Saturday afternoon. It's no surprise that they can come out sloppy and strident. I was in the host's dressing room between dress rehearsal and air—feeling like Stallone, but without the cigar or the nice teeth. I just wanted the show to be good. I needed a punchier ending to the Hillary Clinton Update piece, and my friend and makeup artist Richard Dean suggested "Bitch is the new black." It made sense in the context of the piece and was certainly punchy. Also, it was about 11:10 P.M., so yeah, let's go with that.

I would have chosen to stop short of being overtly political if I'd had more time to smooth it out, because one: I think it's more powerful for comedians and news anchors to be impartial, and two: I am a coward.

The next day Obama supporters on the Huffington Post were outraged. Former president Clinton called me at home to thank me. Mrs. Clinton called later that same day to thank me, proving that Bill is just a tiny bit better at the flash-charm-handshake part of politics.

When I told my mom that former president Clinton told me I "did a great thing for my country" in defending Mrs. Clinton like that, she made a barfing sound. Did I mention that my parents are Republicans?

Friday came, and I know what you're wondering — yes, the Imaginext pirate ship and sea monster I had ordered did arrive, and I wrapped them in my dressing room between setups. I shot for twelve hours at the fake 30 Rock, then, after inspecting the cleanliness of Oprah's airplane set and dressing room for the next morning,* I headed over to the real 30 Rock at about ten P.M. to rehearse with Amy Poehler. I took comfort knowing that Amy could carry the sketch if I stunk it up, because she's such a skilled and generous performer. I mean, she's no Kattan in a dress, but considering the Darwinian limitations on women in comedy, she does very well for herself.

---

* This is not something I would normally do, but I wanted everything to be perfect for Miss Oprah. Jon Hamm, if you come back, I will not be pre-inspecting your toilet. I may inspect it afterward to make sure you didn't steal anything.

We went out on the studio floor in front of the crew, and I tentatively tried out my half-baked impression. Not the worst. Significant room for improvement.

Because Seth and I had written for real impressionists like Darrell Hammond over the years, we knew there were certain tricks we could employ. Whatever sounds are helpful to the impression, you use as many of them as possible in the writing. For Palin it was a lot of "hard R's." Words like "reporters and commentators." Words you can't say, you avoid. For example, I've never been able to figure out how she says "Todd." Amy added jokes. I added some jokes. The whole process was pleasant and collaborative and easy.

Saturday, September 13, I got up at six A.M. and filmed my scenes with Oprah at Silvercup Studios in Queens. She was great. She really does smell nice. And I got to hug her a lot in the scenes. (If you're not into iTunes, you can buy *30 Rock* on DVD at your local Walmart.) Between setups I sat with my daughter on my lap and watched Governor Palin on YouTube and tried to improve my accent. Oprah seemed genuinely concerned for me. "How much rehearsal time are you going to get?" "Do you have tapes of her to listen to?" "You're going there right after this?!" (By the way, when Oprah Winfrey is suggesting you may have overextended yourself, you need to examine your fucking life.) Around 5:30 P.M., Oprah and I wrapped and I went over to *SNL*, but not before stealing an untouched Edible Arrangements® bouquet from Oprah's dressing room to serve at the birthday party the next day.

The rest of the night went thusly: I got to *SNL*, I tried

on my wig and outfit, Amy and I did the sketch three times — run-through, dress rehearsal, and live — and that was it. By 11:40 P.M., I had the rest of the show to relax and have a glass of wine. It was actually the first night out my husband and I had in months.

The whole experience was surprisingly serene. Maybe it was because the Oprah footage was "in the can" and my heart could stop eating itself. Maybe it was because I was safe at the side of my sweet friend Amy. Maybe it was because I knew I couldn't get fired because I didn't even work there anymore anyway. Obviously a big part of it was that Seth had written a very good sketch. I was not nervous at all, and doing that sketch on live TV was a pure joy I had never before experienced as a performer.

Here is the sketch...

ALL REVISED SAT. 2:30PM

(MEYERS)   *1

PALIN/CLINTON COLD OPEN ~ Tina Fey/Amy/~~Pardo~~ Bill V.O.

(OPEN ON: STILL FF: ~~TBA~~ GRAPHIC)
                ~~PARDO~~ BILL (V.O.)(1/4")
                non-partisan
         And now a message from Governor

         Sarah Palin and Senator Hillary Clinton.

(CUT TO: AMY, AS HILLARY
CLINTON AND TINA, AS SARAH
PALIN AT TWO PODIUMS. TINA IS
ENTHUSIASTIC. AMY, LESS SO)

              TINA   AMY

         Thank you!   Thanks.

                   TINA (CONTD)

         Good evening, my fellow Americans.

         I was so excited when I was told

         Senator Clinton and I would be

         addressing you tonight.

                         (MORE)

                    AMY

And I was told I would be

addressing you alone.

                    TINA

Now I know it must be a little

bit strange for all of you to

see the two of us together.

What with me being John McCain's

running mate.

                    AMY

And me being a fervent supporter

of Senator ~~of~~ Barack Obama -- as

evidenced by this button.

                    TINA

But tonight we are crossing

party lines to address the now

very ugly role that sexism is

playing in the campaign.

                    AMY

An issue which I am frankly

surprised to hear people

suddenly care about.

                    (MORE)

                    TINA

You know, Hillary and I don't
agree on everything.

                    AMY

Anything, I believe that diplomacy should
be the cornerstone of any
foreign policy.

                    TINA

And I can see Russia from my house.

                    AMY

I believe global warming is
caused by man.

                    TINA

And I believe it's just God
hugging us closer.

                    AMY

I don't agree with the Bush Doctrine.

                    TINA

And I don't know what that is.

                    AMY

But the one thing we <u>can</u> agree on
is that <u>sexism</u> can never be allowed
to permeate an American election.

                    (MORE)

212 · Tina Fey

PALIN/CLINTON COLD OPEN (CONTD)   **4

          TINA

So please, stop photoshopping my

head on sexy bikini pictures.

          AMY

And stop saying I have ~~fat ankles~~ cankles.

          TINA

Don't refer to me as a MILF.

          AMY

And don't refer to me as a "FLURJ."

I googled what it stands for and ~~it~~ I do

~~is very offensive.~~ not like It.

          TINA

~~So we ask~~ reporters and commentators,

stop using words that diminish us, like

"pretty," "attractive," "beautiful."

          AMY

Or "~~battleaxe~~," "harpy," and "harpy," "shrew,"

"boner ~~killer~~." shrinker."

          TINA

While our politics may differ, my

friend and I are both very tough

ladies. You know it reminds me of a

joke we tell in Alaska.

          (MORE)

TINA (CONTD)	AMY
What's the difference...	Lipstick.
between a hockey mom...	Lipstick.
and a pitbull?	Lipstick.

(BEAT)

Lipstick.

                    TINA

Just look how far we've come.

Hillary Clinton, who came so close

to the White House. And me,

Sarah Palin, who is _even_ closer.

Can you believe it, Hillary?

                    AMY

I can not.

                    TINA

It's truly amazing and I think women

everywhere can agree, that no matter

your politics, it's time for a woman

to make it to the White House.

                    (MORE)

PALIN/CLINTON COLD OPEN (CONTD)   **6

                    AMY
                    He's supposed to be.
No. Mine! Mine!

                    ~~TINA~~

~~Senator?~~

                    AMY

I need to say something. I didn't

want a <u>woman</u> to be President. I

wanted to be President and I ~~am a~~ *just happen to be a*

woman. And I don't want to hear

you compare <u>your</u> road to the White

House to <u>my</u> road to the White

House. I scratched and clawed

through mud and barbed wire and

you just glided in on a dog sled

with your pageant sash and Tina

Fey glasses.

                    TINA

~~Thank you, Hillary.~~ What an amazing

time we live in. To think that just

two years ago, I was a small town

mayor of Alaska's crystal meth capitol.

                    (MORE)

Bossypants • 215

<u>PALIN/CLINTON COLD OPEN</u> (CONTD)   **7

> TINA (CONTD)

And now I am just one ~~geriatric~~

heartbeat away from being President

of the United States. It just goes to

show that <u>anyone</u> can be President.

> AMY

Anyone.

> TINA

All you have to do is want it.

> AMY

(LAUGHS)

Yeah, looking back, if I could

change one thing, I should have

<u>wanted</u> it more.

(RIPS OFF PIECE OF PODIUM)

> TINA

So in the next six weeks, I

invite the media to be vigilant

for sexist behavior.

> AMY

Although it is never sexist to question

a female politician's credentials. Please,

ask <u>this</u> one about dinosaurs.

(MORE)

PALIN/CLINTON COLD OPEN (CONTD)   *8-11

> AMY (CONTD)
>
> ~~Because it certainly wasn't a~~
> *In conclusion,*
> ~~few months ago.~~ So I invite the
> media, to grow a pair. And if
> you can't, I will lend you mine.
>
> TINA/AMY
>
> And, live from New York, it's
> Saturday Night!!!

(<u>ROLL</u>: MONTAGE)

(<u>MUSIC</u>: THEME)

(OUT)

TINA
And as we say in Alask

AMY
We say it everywhere.

This sketch easily could have been a dumb catfight between two female candidates. What Seth and Amy wrote, however, was two women speaking out together against sexism in the campaign. In real life these women experienced different sides of the same sexism coin. People who didn't like Hillary called her a ballbuster. People who didn't like Sarah called her Caribou Barbie. People attempted to marginalize these women based on their gender. Amy's line "Although it is never sexist to question female politicians' credentials" was basically the thesis statement for everything we did over the next six weeks. Not that anyone noticed. You all watched a sketch about feminism and you didn't even realize it because of all the jokes. It's like when Jessica Seinfeld puts spinach in kids' brownies. Suckers!

That night's show was watched by ten million people, so I guess that director at The Second City who said the audience "didn't want to see a sketch with two women" can go shit in his hat.

The next day's birthday party was also successful and, I believe, had an equal impact on the 2008 presidential campaign. Special thanks to my sister-in-law Dee, who brought macaroni and cheese, and Jessie, who made jerk chicken. Here is a now-historic photo of my friend Michael's pirate ship cake.

The next few weeks were very exciting. On Wednesday, my daughter started preschool. The Sunday after that, *30 Rock* won seven Emmys. Meanwhile, once a week,

I went to my goof-around night job and did these sketches, and this is what I remember about them.

Week 2: Katie Couric Interviews Sarah Palin

I think Amy would want me to say she's very pregnant in this photo.

Seth had originally written a piece with Sarah Palin "in one," which means by herself, talking straight to the camera. I asked if we could change it so I could be with Amy again. Since my background is improvisation and not stand-up, I really prefer the buddy system on stage. The Katie Couric interview was basically a sketch handed to us on a plate.

Seth quickly wrote a draft, and because I was watching Mrs. Palin over and over again on YouTube to try to improve the impression, I asked Seth if I could put in this long rambling run about the bailout that was mostly just transcribed.

By the second week, I realized what made this experience so fun and different. For the first time ever, I was performing in front of an audience that *wanted* to see me. I had spent so many years handing out fliers, begging people to check out my improv team. I was so used to trying to win the audience over or just get permission to be there that a willing audience was an incredible luxury. It was like having a weight lifted off you. I thought, "This must be what it's like for Darrell when he plays Bill Clinton." Or for Tracy Morgan when he does anything. People are just happy to see them.

Week 3: The Vice Presidential Debate

This was my favorite sketch, and there are three reasons why.

One, I felt like I contributed a lot of jokes to this one, so my writer ego likes it the best.

Two, Queen Latifah was there.

Three, I thought the speeches that Jim Downey wrote for Jason Sudeikis as Joe Biden were brilliant. Especially the stuff where Biden is trying to prove that he's not some Washington elite by talking about how he's from Scranton, Pennsylvania, "the most godforsaken place on earth." I thought that was ingenious, because not only was the ad hominem attack on Scranton a hilarious comedy left turn, it also exemplified what the election had become. Instead of talking about issues, everybody was trying to prove how

"down-home" they were. "I'm just like you" was the subtext of every speech.

Politics and prostitution have to be the only jobs where inexperience is considered a virtue. In what other profession would you brag about not knowing stuff? "I'm not one of those fancy Harvard heart surgeons. I'm just an unlicensed plumber with a dream and I'd like to cut your chest open." The crowd cheers.

Two jokes I remember writing for the debate sketch are this one about global warming:

> Gwen Ifill
> Senator Palin, address your position on
> global warming and whether you think
> it's man-made or not.
>
> Gov. Sarah Palin
> Gwen, we don't know if this climate
> change hoozie-what's-it is man-made
> or if it's just a natural part of the
> "End of Days."

And this one:

```
          Gwen Ifill
Governor Palin, would you extend
same-sex rights to the entire country?

        Gov. Sarah Palin
You know, I would be afraid of where
that would lead. I believe marriage
is meant to be a sacred institution
between two unwilling teenagers.
```

This joke about the "sacred institution of marriage" was probably the roughest joke we did. "Rough" in sketch comedy language means harsh or dark. As I'm sure you remember, Mrs. Palin's daughter Bristol was pregnant at the time and engaged to her high school boyfriend Levi Johnston. This joke was right on the edge of being too directly about the Palin family. I felt, however, that because Bristol's pregnancy and subsequent engagement had been embraced by so many people as a shining example of the pro-life movement, it was officially part of the campaign. Also, the joke wasn't *that* rough. An example of a truly rough joke would be this:

A pedophile walks through the woods with a child. The child says, "These woods are scary." The pedophile says, "Tell me about it. I have to walk back through here alone."

That is a rough joke.
Or:

Sarah Palin: To think that just two years ago, I was a small-town mayor of Alaska's crystal meth capital. And now I am just one weird mole *away from being president of the United States.*

A John McCain skin cancer joke? Too rough. That was a joke I tried in dress rehearsal in the Sarah-Hillary sketch. My friend Jen Rogers, who is a cancer survivor, thought it was funny. The studio audience did not.

I remember very distinctly walking off stage after Latifah yelled "Live from New York," thinking that this was the most fun, exciting thing I would ever do. I remember thinking this was a "permanent win." No one would ever be able to take it away from me. The proof existed permanently on tape that on this one occasion, I was funny.

Here at the midway point of my six-week career, the sketches were really becoming "a thing." They were being watched around the world on the Internet. A French newspaper accidentally ran a picture of Amy and me from the Katie Couric sketch thinking it was a picture of Couric and Palin. Although I think that had less to do with the "power of satire" and more to do with the fact that to the French, we are all indistinguishable fat dough balls.

And Oh, the Cable News Reportage! The great thing about cable news is that they have to have something to talk about twenty-four hours a day. Sometimes it's Anderson Cooper giggling with one of the Real Housewives of Atlanta. Sometimes it's Rick Sanchez screaming about corn syrup. They have endless time to fill, but viewers get kind of "bummed out" if they supply actual information about wars and stuff, so "Media Portrayal of Sarah Palin" and *SNL* and I became the carrageenan in America's news nuggets for several weeks. I was a cable news star, like a shark or a missing white child!

The downside of being a cable news star is that any ass-hair with a clip-on tie can come on as an "expert" to talk about you. One day, by accident, I caught this tool Tom something on MSNBC saying that he thought I had not "conducted myself well" during all this. In his opinion, Mrs. Palin had conducted herself with dignity and I had not. (I'm pretty sure Tom's only claim to expertise is that he oversees a website where people guess incorrectly who might win show biz awards.) There was a patronizing attitude behind Tom's comments that I certainly don't think he would have applied to a male comedian. Chris Rock was touring at the time and he was literally calling George W. Bush "retarded" in his act. I don't think Tom something would have expressed disappointment that Chris was not conducting himself sweetly. I learned how incredibly frustrating it is to watch someone talk smack about you and *not be able to respond.*

This kind of anger, I suspect, is the main thing Mrs. Palin and I have in common. When someone says something bad about us, we want to respond.

However, I, as an experienced member of the East Coast Media Elite, know that you can't even try. You can rage to your spouse all you want, but the moment you post Internet comments under an assumed name, or call in spontaneously to a radio show to assert that you are *not* "a butterface," or write that letter to Lisa de Moraes of the *Washington Post* instructing her to "go suck a bag of dicks," you have crossed the border into Crazytown, never to return.

Around This Time...

Around this time my old friend Damian Holbrook, a writer for *TV Guide,* had arranged to interview me for the new fall season. (Damian and I did Summer Showtime together.* I named the character Damian in *Mean Girls* after him.)

He spent the day on the *30 Rock* set and came over to my apartment for dinner afterward. Damian has a great sense of humor and we laughed a lot. After dinner—long after what I considered the "interview portion" of our day to be over—Damian asked me what I would do if McCain-Palin won the election. Would I continue to moonlight at *SNL?* I said in a jokey, actress-y voice, "If they win, I will leave Earth." It was clearly a joke about people who say stupid things like that. No matter what your political beliefs, everyone knows some loudmouth: "If Bush wins, I'm moving to *Canada.*" "If Bush wins again, I am seriously moving to Canada." "If Obama wins, I'm going to shoot that *#%*@." Etc.

But Damian put "I'm leaving Earth" in his article, and in print it looked sincerely idiotic. His editor leaked it in advance of the issue to generate attention for the magazine.

---

* See if you can guess what I changed his name to in that chapter.

Cable news took the bait and ran with it. I looked like a grade A dummy. I was annoyed at Damian, but mostly I just found it disconcerting. That I could get in "trouble" for a half-baked joke I made in my own home was a level of scrutiny I did not enjoy.

My brother called me, genuinely concerned. I should watch what I was saying because there are "a lot of nuts out there." I hung up the phone and burst into tears in the *30 Rock* writers' room. Poor Matt Hubbard watched my meltdown with a look of concern and disgust usually reserved for watching your mom vomit.

Week 4: Weekend Update Prime-Time Special with Will Ferrell

SNL was doing half-hour specials on Thursday nights at 8:30. I was able to be in one, in what can only be described as "My Trip to Sketch Comedy Fantasy Camp." I got to stand next to Will Ferrell as George W. Bush and Darrell Hammond as John McCain. These two dudes are the masters. Darrell is a precise technician who can do anyone from Jesse Jackson to Donald Trump to Al Gore. Will, on the other hand, is an impressionist in the style of the Impressionists. His technique is loose, bordering on random, but when you step back he has rendered George W. Bush.

If Darrell is da Vinci, Will is Monet, and I am me, in a wig.

This sketch had a different tone than the other sketches because it was written by the world's number one comic genius, Adam McKay (*Anchorman, Talladega Nights*). It was about George W. Bush trying to endorse the McCain-Palin ticket and John McCain trying to avoid the endorsement.

It's worth pointing out that this sketch was the tipping point for my Republican parents. They had been as excited and entertained as anyone for the first few weeks. Maybe the tone of this sketch was more aggressive, or maybe the cable news cycle had worn them down into thinking we were being mean, but the end result was a scolding from my mom: "It's getting to be too much now."

Week 5: The "Sneaker Upper"

"Sneaker Upper" is a term that veteran *SNL* writer Jim Downey coined to describe that queer moment when a famous person "sneaks up" behind the actor who plays them and pretends to be mad about it. I would expand

Jim's definition to include any time someone being parodied volunteers to come on the show and prove they're "in on the joke." Comedy writers hate Sneaker Uppers. On a pure writing level, it's just lame. But like other lame things—sorbet, line dancing, New Year's Eve—people seem to love it. I'm not saying I'm above a Sneaker Upper. During my time at *SNL* I was involved in at least five of these things. They varied in success and included people ranging from Debbie Matenopoulos to Monica Lewinsky.

If you were having a Sneaker Upper week, your coworkers would ask sympathetically, "How's *that* going?" What could you do? Some weeks you got to produce a pure little comedy piece that was dear to your heart and had a great host like Alec Baldwin or Julia Louis-Dreyfus in it. Some weeks you had to sit and take notes from the smallest Hanson brother about what jokes he didn't care for. The Sneaker Upper is just an occupational hazard, and as occupational hazards go, it's much better than getting your arm caught in the thresher.

What I'm getting to is, during week five, Sarah Palin's campaign people called Lorne to say she'd like to be on the show. I was against it.

One, it was a classic Sneaker Upper, and we had been so successful on a writing level up to that point.

Two, things were getting tense. McCain-Palin supporters were yelling racist invective at rallies, and the campaign wasn't exactly shutting that behavior down. I didn't want to joke around and hug her on camera and be perceived as endorsing their campaign.

Three, I had seen footage of Governor Palin and her

sweet littlest daughter, Piper, getting booed at a Flyers game. (Classy, hometown, real classy.) I was sure that the liberal NYC studio audience for *SNL* would boo the shit out of her. I didn't want that to happen and I definitely didn't want to stand next to her while that happened and have it seem like we had laid a trap for her. I didn't want to be complicit in an ugly live-TV moment during what was becoming an increasingly ugly campaign.

Lorne didn't think it would be a problem. However, Lorne was also riding three weeks of 7+ ratings, and the real Mrs. Palin would surely exceed that. She was ratings gold—pure nuggets of "ratings gold" just waiting to be extracted from the teeth of a corpse. (In this metaphor I'm not sure if the corpse represents my career, the McCain campaign, or broadcast television.)

I told Lorne that if the real governor did the show, I would sit this one out. Lorne suggested I not decide so quickly. He and I both knew that things had gotten so weird in the cable news cycle that if I didn't show up, it would be just as much of a fake news story. The CNN crawl would have read, "MEAN GIRL: Fey refuses to appear with Palin. Palin supporters call the move 'un-American' and 'vaguely Jewish.' Tonight at 9 EST Rick Sanchez uncovers the Corn Syrup Myth . . ."

It really was a catch-22 for me, unless Lorne would just decline to have her on. And that wasn't going to happen. See above re: ratings gold.

I was hurt that Lorne would put me in this position. At the same time, it is never lost on me that he also "put me in the position" of being on TV in the first place, which no one else in the world would have done. Trust me, I used to audition for things.

I called Lorne and said I would do the show but that it was very important to me that we protect Governor Palin from being booed. I suggested that he start with her backstage in the 8H hallway. The live audience would only see her on the monitors and, not knowing if what they were seeing was live or pretaped, they would be less likely to boo.

My only other request was this: I never wanted to appear in a "two shot" with Mrs. Palin. I mean, she really is taller and better looking than I am, and we would literally be wearing the same outfit. I'd already been made to stand next to Jennifer Aniston and Salma Hayek on camera in my life; a gal can only take so much. And honestly, I knew that if that picture existed, it would be what they show on the Emmys someday when I die, and I'd really rather they show this picture.

Lorne called back the next day to say he had an idea and Seth was working on a draft. We'd start with me in a fake press conference, then cut to Lorne and Governor Palin backstage. It was Lorne's idea to have Alec Baldwin there, too.

As a beloved *SNL* host and a known liberal crusader, Alec standing next to Sarah would send out an "everybody be cool" message to the audience.

We rehearsed on Saturday afternoon as usual, but this time there was massive security in the building for the vice presidential nominee. I met Mrs. Palin on the studio floor when we came out to rehearse. She was in full hair and makeup because she'd come straight from a campaign stop. I had my hair in a ponytail and looked my trademark exhausted. We shook hands and I blurted out, "Don't worry, they'll put makeup on me." As we took our places to rehearse, my daughter pointed animatedly at Governor Palin on the monitor. "She's confused," Mrs. Palin laughed.

We didn't hang out much, but we chatted a little about children. She offered her daughter Bristol to babysit Alice during the show if need be. I thanked her, saying Alice was too little to stay for the show. She always went home with her dad after the dinner break. I can't imagine Bristol would have been too psyched to do that anyway; it was her eighteenth birthday, she was in New York City, and I had made a vicious joke about her a week earlier. But I appreciated the mom-ness of Mrs. Palin's offer. She might as well have said, "You guys need to take these sets down tonight? Cuz I can get Todd down here with a Makita."

Mrs. Palin's whole camp was helpful. Her hairstylist made adjustments to my wig to make it even more like the governor's hair. Her makeup artist identified the lip color that we'd been trying to figure out for four weeks: It was just lip liner, under Chapstick.

And then it was 11:30.

Seth wrote an admirable Sneaker Upper. Some solid jokes at the top, and Alec was funny with her backstage. There was the requisite amount of sweaty feigned surprise.

Governor Palin and I crossed paths for just an instant, and when she took center stage she was greeted with a long round of applause. I'd like to think that my suggestion of starting her backstage paid off, but more likely I had underestimated what a giant media star Sarah Palin was; even the New Yorkiest audience was giddy to see her in person.

After the show I felt compelled to find Mrs. Palin in her dressing room and say good-bye. "Good job. You should come back and host sometime," I said. She certainly could handle it. And then, "Now, you're gonna tell everyone you had a good time in New York City, right? And that everyone was really nice to you?" Mrs. Palin smiled and nodded. "Yep. Nobody was scary or anything." I couldn't believe the condescension that was coming out of my mouth. I was talking to this woman like I was reminding a child to say "please." I guess I was just hoping that wherever the campaign took her the next day, she would include New York City as one of the "pro-America" parts of her country.

In my opinion, the most meaningful moment for women in the 2008 campaign was not Governor Palin's convention speech or Hillary Clinton conceding her 1,896 delegates. The moment most emblematic of how things have changed for women in America was nine-months-pregnant Amy Poehler rapping as Sarah Palin and tearing the roof off the place.

Watching Amy rap made me so happy that she had found a way to make real comedy out of a Sneaker Upper. The virtuosity and joyfulness of her performance made me feel like it was time for me to hand this job back to the professionals. I felt like that character in *Flowers for Algernon*. Not Charlie, the lady teacher from the college who realizes, "I've got to stop dry-humping this mentally challenged guy!"

The rating was a 10.7 / 14 million people.

One More Weird Time, and That's It?

The week before the election, John McCain wanted to come on the show. I had met Senator McCain when he hosted *SNL* in 2002, and we all liked him very much. (He was not one of the unnamed d-bags.) I had even spent a day with him in DC. He gave my husband and me a tour of the Senate before we posed together for this "get out the vote" cover of *Life* magazine.

(The magazine went under immediately after this, by the way.)

Did it seem insane that a presidential candidate would want to appear in a sketch parodying his running mate just days before the election? Sure, but what didn't seem insane then? A Kenyan Communist Muslim was about to be elected president. Seth wrote a sketch about McCain-Palin buying time on QVC as a last-ditch effort to reach voters.

For the last time* Jane the makeup artist overdrew my lips to make my mouth look wider. Louis glued my ears down (my ears stick out and Sarah's don't) and Betty

---

* It wasn't the last time, apparently. Also, I am available for parties and corporate events.

popped on my long brown wig. I went to Senator McCain's dressing room to read through the cue cards with him, and he started laughing uncomfortably when he saw me. "It's just weird," he said.

And that was it. We had gone through the entire life cycle of an *SNL* character—from first-time jitters to Sneaker Upper to "This again?"—in six weeks.

One of the best parts of all this is that my daughter may actually have childhood memories of going to *SNL*. I left so soon after she was born, I didn't think she would know that place or those people, but now she will, which means a lot to me because that was my home for a long time.

One of the worst parts of all of this was that I learned what it felt like to be a lightning rod. I got some hate mail, and there are definitely people out there who will dislike me for the rest of my life because of "what I did" to Sarah Palin. On an intellectual level, this doesn't bother me at all. On a human level, I would prefer to be liked. There was an assumption that I was personally attacking Sarah Palin by impersonating her on TV. No one ever said it was "mean" when Chevy Chase played Gerald Ford falling down all the time. No one ever accused Dana Carvey or Darrell Hammond or Dan Aykroyd of "going too far" in their political impressions. You see what I'm getting at here. I am not mean and Mrs. Palin is not fragile. To imply otherwise is a disservice to us both.

A few months after our friendly chat about kids (and my condescending remarks about New York), Mrs. Palin told conservative filmmaker John Ziegler that Katie Couric and I had exploited and profited by her family. But I know better than to respond to attacks in the media. Although if I *were* to respond, I would probably just say, "Nice reality show." Or maybe I'd point out that when those sketches were watched 58 million times on the Internet around the world, I was paid nothing because actors don't get any money for Internet reuse. (Get ready for an actors' strike in 2012.) But I'd probably just know better than to respond.

Some may argue that exploiting Governor Palin and her family helped bring attention to my low-rated TV show. I am proud to say you are wrong. My TV show still enjoys very low ratings. In fact, I think the Palin stuff may have hurt the TV show. Let's face it, between Alec Baldwin and me there is a certain fifty percent of the population who think we are pinko Commie monsters.

There's a Drunk Midget
in My House

Ah, babies! They're more than just adorable little crea-
tures on whom you can blame your farts. Like most
people who have had one baby, I am an expert on everything and will tell you, unsolicited, how to raise your kid!

Breast-feeding v. Formula

Invented in the mid-1800s as a last-ditch option for orphans
and underweight babies, packaged infant formula has
since been perfected to be a complete and reliable source
of stress and shame for mothers. Anyone who reads a pregnancy book knows that breast milk provides nutrition,
immunities, and invaluable bonding time. The breast is
best. Unless you need to get back on your psych meds or
something, in which case give your baby Crystal Light on
the Go or whatever it takes for you to not go crazy.

But if you're healthy, you really should nurse. *You owe
it to your baby to breast-feed.*

When I was pregnant (remember, I was pregnant once, *and* I'm on TV: Those two things combined make me an *expert*) I was confused as to why all the literature about breast-feeding was surrounded by ads for formula.

The free magazines in my doctor's office all said the same thing in their articles: "Breast-feeding is best for your baby." But overwhelming those articles were pages of heartwarming full-color ads saying things like:

"Your baby deserves the best. INFAMILK, now with more Crypthecodinium!"

"DOCTORS SAY breastfeed or if you're an adoptive mother TRY SIMIMIL."

"10 out of 100,000 doctors say Enfante probably doesn't cause blindness."

"No other formula gives your baby a better start in life except that stuff that comes out of you for free."

Should I breast-feed or not? I asked my mother for advice. "Don't even try it," she said. This is a generational difference. This is the same woman who told me to request "twilight sleep" during delivery. (Twilight sleep is the memory-erasing pain medication that doctors gave women in the 1950s whenever they had to take a baby out or put a body snatcher in.) I could *never* have chosen twilight sleep because I wanted to be present for my birth experience and also it is no longer offered. My mom is a Depression baby. As a member of Generation X, I was more informed, more empowered, and I knew that when it came to breast-feeding I had an obligation to my baby to pretend to try.

I chose to breast-feed, and it was an *amazing* time in my life. It really changed me as a woman, and it's the most gratifying thing I've ever done.*

There are a lot of different opinions as to how long one should breast-feed. The World Health Organization says six months. The American Association of Pediatrics says one year is ideal. *Mothering* magazine suggests you nurse the child until just before his rehearsal dinner. I say you must find what works for you. For my little angel and me the magic number was about seventy-two hours.

We began our breast-feeding journey in the hospital under the tutelage of an encouraging Irish night nurse named Mary. We tried the football hold, the cross-cradle hold, and one I like to call the Bret Michaels, where you kind of lie over the baby and stick your breast in its mouth to wake it up. We didn't succeed, so that first night the other nurses gave my little one some formula without asking. I tried to be appalled, but I was pretty tired. Once we got home, we tried again. I abandoned all vanity, as one must, and parked it shirtless on the couch. Here we experienced another generational difference. Gen X wanted to succeed at this so she could tell people she did it, and little Gen Z wanted me to hand over that goddamn formula, and she was willing to scream until she got it.

One of my five hundred nicknames for my daughter is Midge, which is short for Midget, because she was a very small baby. She was born a week early and a little underweight at five pounds seven ounces. My obstetrician suggested the next day at her bedside visit that perhaps I

---

* Except for several very satisfying work-related things.

hadn't rested enough during my pregnancy and that was why she was so small. "What a cunt," I thought to myself in what was either a flash of postpartum hormones or an accurate assessment of my doctor's personality.*

So we started supplementing Midge regularly with formula. She was small and I didn't want her to get any smaller while I mastered the ancient art of breast-feeding to prove how incredible and impressive I am. Of course, I still provided her breast milk. You must, must, must provide them with breast milk. *You owe it to your baby to get them that breast milk.* Here's how it works.

If you choose to not love your baby enough to breast-feed, you can pump your milk using a breast pump. (This may be easier for the modern mom because it is an expensive appliance and we're more comfortable with those than with babies.) Set up a pumping ritual for yourself that is relaxing and consistent. I chose to pump every two hours while watching episodes of the HBO series *Entourage* On Demand. Over the whir of the milking machine, I could almost hear my baby being lovingly cared for in the other room while Turtle yelled across an SUV, "Yo E, you ever fuck a girl while she has her period?" I was able to do this for almost seven weeks before running out of *Entourage* episodes and sinking into a deep depression.

Shortly thereafter, we made the switch to an all-formula diet. If you've ever opened a can of infant formula mix,

* Lest this seem like an overreaction, she also said, "The nurse and I were laughing at you that you had to push so long to deliver such a small baby."

then you know it smells like someone soaked old vitamins in a bucket of wet leaves, then dried them in a hot car. Also, formula is like forty dollars a can. They keep it locked up behind the counter with the batteries and meth ingredients. That's how bad people want this stuff!

However, the baby was thriving. I was no longer feeling trapped, spending thirty out of every ninety minutes attached to a Williams-Sonoma Tit Juicer. But I still had an overwhelming feeling of disappointment. I had failed at something that was supposed to be natural.

I was defensive and grouchy whenever the topic came up. At a party with a friend who was successfully nursing her little boy, I watched her husband produce a bottle of pumped breast milk that was the size of a Big Gulp. It was more milk than I had produced in my whole seven weeks—I blame *Entourage*. As my friend's husband fed the baby, he said offhandedly, "This stuff is liquid gold. You know it actually makes them smarter?" "Let's set a date!" I screamed. "IQ test. Five years from today. My formula baby will crush your baby!" Thankfully, my mouth was so full of cake they could not understand me.

Once I let go of my guilt, which took a while, the only remaining obstacle was the Teat Nazis. These are the women who not only brag endlessly about how much their five year old still loves breast milk, but they also grill you about your choices. You can recognize the TNs by their hand-carved daggers:

"Are you breast-feeding? Isn't it amazing? I really think it's how I lost the weight so easily. Did you have a vaginal birth? I went natural and I didn't even tear. Are you back at work already? Do you feel weird about going back to work? I just love my baby so much I can't imagine going back to work yet. You're not nursing? She's only fifteen months; you should try again!"

Now, let me be clear; millions of women around the world nurse their children beautifully for years without giving anybody else a hard time about it. Teat Nazis are a solely western upper-middle-class phenomenon occurring when highly ambitious women experience deprivation from outside modes of achievement. Their highest infestation pockets are in Brooklyn and Hollywood.

If you are confronted by a TN, you have two options. One, when they ask if you're breast-feeding, you can smile and say, "Yes. It's amazing." *(You owe it to your baby to lie.)* Or you can go for the kill. The only people who can shame the Teat Nazis are the Adoptive Mommies. If you have a friend who has an adopted child, especially one from another country, *bring him or her around,* because they make the Teat Nazis' brains short-circuit: "How can I... feel superior...you...bigger sacrifice...can't judge..." and their big ol' dinner plate nipples pop off as they crumple to the ground and disappear.

Lesson learned? When people say, "You really, really *must*" do something, it means you don't really have to. No one ever says, "You really, really *must* deliver the baby during labor." When it's true, it doesn't need to be said.

"Me Time"

*A*ny expert will tell you, the best thing a mom can do to be a better mom is to carve out a little time for herself. Here are some great "me time" activities you can do.

Go to the bathroom a lot.

Offer to empty the dishwasher.

Take ninety-minute showers. (If you only shower every three or four days, it will be easier to get away with this.)

Say you're going to look for the diaper crème, then go into your child's room and just stand there until your spouse comes in and curtly says, "What are you doing?"

Stand over the sink and eat the rest of your child's dinner while he or she pulls at your pant leg asking for it back.

Try to establish that you're the only one in your family allowed to go to the post office.

"Sleep when your baby sleeps." Everyone knows this classic tip, but I say why stop there? Scream when your baby screams. Take Benadryl when your baby takes Benadryl. And walk around pantless when your baby walks around pantless.

Read! When your baby is finally down for the night, pick up a juicy book like Eat, Pray, Love or Pride and Prejudice or my personal favorite, Understanding Sleep Disorders: Narcolepsy and Apnea; A Clinical Study. *Taking some time to read each night really taught me how to feign narcolepsy when my husband asked me what my "plan" was for taking down the Christmas tree.*

Just implementing four or five of these little techniques will prove restorative and give you the energy you need to not drink until nighttime.

A Celebrity's Guide to Celebrating the Birth of Jesus

Goldie and Kurt like to soak in the crystal blue waters of St. Barts. Melanie and Antonio prefer the festive chill of Aspen. Tina and Jeff are absolutely mad for Route 80W between Philadelphia and Youngstown! We never miss it.

Lying on a beach feels a little "first thought" to me. I prefer the retro chic of spending Christmas just like Joseph and Mary did—traveling arduously back to the place of your birth to be counted, with no guarantee of a bed when you get there. You may end up sleeping on an old wicker couch with a dog licking your face while an Ab Rocket infomercial plays in the background. It's a modern-day manger.

Our annual pilgrimage from one set of in-laws to the other happens every December 26, or, as they call it in Canada: Boring Day.

We always plan to leave around seven in the morning and, like clockwork, we're out the door by ten. After gassing up, deicing, and turning around for an unanticipated bowel movement, we glide onto glorious 80W by ten thirty. Sure, there are those trendy types who prefer 76/70 because it's "more scenic" and "they have a McDonald's," but I think 80W has a certain *ceci me déprime*.

My husband drives the whole seven hours because I don't have a driver's license. It's just one of the many ways in which I am developmentally stunted. I don't drive. I can't cook meat correctly. *And* I have no affinity for animals. I don't hate animals and I would never hurt an animal; I just don't actively care about them. When a coworker shows me cute pictures of her dog, I struggle to respond correctly, like an autistic person who has been taught to recognize human emotions from flash cards. In short, I am the worst.

There are plenty of *positives* to being married to me. I just can't think of any of them right now, and I'm sure my husband can't think of any of them either while he's driving wideways across Pennsylvania.

Still: There's something hypnotic and relaxing about cruising through the Alleghenies, frantically searching for a radio signal. If traffic is moving well, you won't ever find a station that lasts for an entire song. So you nestle in between your baking-hot dashboard and the freezing-cold door and enjoy the radio's static with occasional fragments of a shouted religious broadcast.

KHHHHHHHHHHHHHHHH—Friends, are you living in such a way that there is a crown in heaven waiting for you?—KHHHHHHHHHHHHHHHHHH- HHHHHHHHHH—a man must die of self—

KHHHHHHHHHHHHHHHHHHHHHHHHHHHH-
HHHHHHHHHHHHHH.

When you feel about to "die of self," pull over and enjoy one of the local eateries.

I recommend the Roy Rogers at Exit 4B or the Roy Rogers at Exit 78. If you're a die-hard "foodie," hop off the road in DuBois and enjoy a Subway sandwich made at a place that is eighty percent gas station.

"Youngstown!" my husband always yells as we pass the sign. He yells it in a way that you can actually hear the letters getting bigger at the end like an old-timey postcard. It never fails to startle me and make me laugh. Half the time it wakes me up. Yes, I fall asleep while he's driving. Did I mention that I'm the worst?

In the last hour, highway turns to snowy country roads and the GPS system shuts down because you're in a part of the world that Toyota doesn't recognize (and the feeling is mutual).

We always pull up carefully, making sure not to run over any outdoor cats. (One of the best-kept secrets of "country life" is that people accidentally crush their own pets a lot.)

The house is cozy warm from the wood-burning heater. There are hugs and kisses and pies and soup and ham and biscuits and a continuous flow of Maxwell House coffee with nondairy creamer. We City Folk can pretend that we prefer the rotgut from Starcorps with skim milk and Splenda, but who are we kidding? Maxwell House with French vanilla corn syrup cannot be beat.

If there's one thing my husband's hometown has that St. Barts does not, it's the water. "Legally potable" doesn't quite capture it. Straight from the tap it smells like... How can I describe it? — if you boiled ten thousand eggs in a prostitute's bathwater. It turns your jewelry green, but it leaves your hair soft and manageable. So, while I couldn't *find* it in St. Barts, I could probably *sell* it there.

My in-laws always have a huge dog—a dog so big that even I can see it. For years it was Robbie. When Robbie passed away from surprisingly non-vehicle-related causes, they got Bear. Another way my body rejects dog love is that I am allergic to them. Those first few Christmases, I had to dose myself with Benadryl to survive. I would end up sleeping half the day and then shuffling aimlessly around the house like later-years Judy Garland in a Christmas special. Most of my in-laws didn't experience my actual personality until Claritin was invented. By then it was too late to get rid of me.

My three sisters-in-law have always been welcoming and affectionate, and boy, can they clean a kitchen. After a big family meal they rinse and scrape and dry and Saranwrap like nobody's business. I pitch in half-assedly like the spoiled suburban younger child that I am. "Where... should I put... this... chicken bone? Throw it out, or...?" See above, re: "worst."

I can't promise you will find a family as lovely as my in-laws to stay with on your Route 80 Christmas. Honestly, I know you won't, because we had Mamaw Pearline. Pearline was eighty-seven when I met her and she lived to be ninety-six. She spent almost all her time upstairs in the den watching TV and chain-smoking. She had gradually retired from working hard all her life, raising kids, cleaning, and cooking in a coal camp in West Virginia. She had earned the right to refer to the *National Enquirer* as "the newspaper."

By the time my daughter was born, Pearline's short-term memory was gone. She'd come downstairs and smile at the baby. "Whose little baby is this?" "IT'S JEFF'S!" we'd yell. "Look at those dark eyebrows." She'd smile and pat the baby's head. "I never saw a baby with such dark eyebrows!" Then, two hours later, she'd come down for a cup of coffee. "Whose little baby is this? Look at those dark eyebrows!" This went on for three days.

For reference, this is the swarthy little baby she was talking about.

We did seven or eight 80W Christmases in a row before I had to be a fool and mess with perfection. Why couldn't I be like Goldie and Kurt and stick with what works? I couldn't because as glamorous as the drive always was, it got even more magical and glamorous when the baby became a toddler. One year, I believe, she screamed all the way from Hazleton to the Moshannon State Forest. And who could blame her? She didn't understand why we had strapped her into this frozen contraption only to shove cold Roy Rogers fries in her mouth.

In an attempt to make things easier for myself, which is the basis for all of history's worst decisions (see: "George W. Bush's Repeal of the Estate Tax," "Scott Peterson's Plan," and *"Dred Scott v. Sandford"*), I invited the whole family out to New York for a Christmas adventure. I learned quickly that trying to force Country Folk to love the Big City is like telling your gay cousin, "You just haven't met the right girl yet." They just don't like big cities. It's okay. It's natural. They were born that way.

When you see your Big City through a non-admirer's eyes you notice things you normally would not.

"Hmm. I guess there *are* a lot of dog turds on Eighty-third Street."

"No, it's great. We just put our garbage out the back door and when it starts to overflow the super picks it up."

"Who, *that* guy? Yeah...he's playing with himself. Okay, let's go in the playground the other way."

The Christmas in New York Adventure didn't go so

well. My father-in-law tripped on a crack in the pavement and spent the rest of the week politely pretending he had not dislocated his shoulder. I dragged all the kids onto the subway and through the crowd to see the Rockefeller Center Christmas tree, which is unlike any tree in the world, except for hundreds of trees near their homes in Ohio.

If I had one bone to pick with the Country Folks, it's that they are not gastronomically adventurous. Family-style Italian sent them all running for the Alka-Seltzer. Greek yogurt left my sister-in-law stymied, like I had offered her a bowl of caulk. But who am I to judge? I have never been able to get my head around ham salad or pickled eggs. And I would like it explained to me in writing what's so great about apple butter.

After four days, I could see the city wearing them down. It was too much walking for them, oddly. It turns out City Folk walk way more than Country Folk.

My young nephew went to the deli with me. "There sure are a lot of foreigners here." No, I explained, those people live here. In the "Great American Melting Pot," rural Ohio may be a lump of white flour that hasn't been stirred properly. Not that New York is any better. New York is that chunk of garlic that you bite into thinking it's potato and you can't get the taste out of your mouth all day. It all blends once you mix it, but sometimes you really have to grind it against the side.

Clearly we needed to shake that year off and try something new. Last year, determined to "save" the full 80W drive until our daughter can really *appreciate* it in twenty years or so, I made a new pitch: Let's meet in the middle. We chose Williamsport, Pennsylvania, home of the Little League World Series and almost exactly halfway between us on the map.

We'd spend three days and two nights at the Holiday Inn and then head our separate ways. I cannot emphasize to you how well this went...because I don't know how to do "double underline" on my computer.

The kids swam in the hotel pool. We dined at Red Lobster. There is no one of-woman-born who does not like Red Lobster cheddar biscuits. Anyone who claims otherwise is a liar and a Socialist. We fed fifteen people for two hundred dollars. Success!

The next day, while Beyoncé and Jay-Z were probably having a frustrating time on their yacht trying to figure out the French word for plunger, we walked around the Lycoming Mall. There was a carousel for the kids. Later, we exchanged gifts in the lobby by a ten-foot Christmas tree that none of us had to put up or take down. Victory!

That night, while Mariah and Nick shopped for dog jewelry in Aspen, we convened for an amazing meal at a local inn called the Herdic House. This stately Victorian inn offered a menu where city jerks and country carnivores could find common ground. Pork chops, duck, pear crisp. The setting was cozy and twinkly and Christmassy in a way that worked for everybody.

Of course the final ingredient for a perfect Christmas vacation is a good Buffer. A Buffer is a neutral party who keeps the conversation light. Everyone needs a Buffer. You don't think Mary and Joseph were psyched to see the Little Drummer Boy?

That night at the Herdic House my best friend from high school, Marlene, and her husband joined us for the evening. She was visiting family in Williamsport, too, and she is the perfect Buffer. My girl Marlene can talk to *anyone*. She could talk to a Frankenstein about neck bolts. She could talk to your great-aunt Joyce about the tumors of a person she has never met. She could exchange e-mail addresses with a wreath. Nick and Mariah *wish* they had a Buffer this good. They probably wanted to kill each other after three days of wearing matching ski outfits and never skiing. WILLIAMSPORT FOR THE WIN!

This Christmas I'll be riding my metaphorical donkey all the way across 80W again. But I'm insisting that we're back in New York City for New Year's Eve, where we do more of an Ahab-and-Jezebel thing.

Juggle This

My daughter recently checked out a book from the preschool library called *My Working Mom*. It had a cartoon witch on the cover. "Did you pick this book out all by yourself?" I asked her, trying to be nonchalant. Yes. We read the book and the witch mother was very busy and sometimes reprimanded her daughter for messing things up near her cauldron. She had to fly away to a lot of meetings, and the witch's child said something like, "It's hard having a working mom, especially when she enjoys her work." In the heartwarming conclusion, the witch mother makes it to the child's school play at the last second, and the witch's child says she doesn't like having a working mom but she can't picture her mom any other way. I didn't love it. I'm sure the TWO MEN who wrote this book had the absolute best intentions, but this leads me to my point. The topic of working moms is a tap dance recital in a minefield.

It is less dangerous to draw a cartoon of Allah French-kissing Uncle Sam—which let me make it very clear I

HAVE NOT DONE—than it is to speak honestly about this topic.

I will start by saying that I have once or twice been offered a "mother of the year" award by working-mom groups or a mommy magazine, and I always decline. How could they possibly know if I'm a good mother? How can any of us know until the kid is about thirty-three and all the personality dust has really settled? But working moms want to validate that it's okay to work, especially if they work at magazines where they can then package that validation and sell it to stay-at-home moms who are craving news from the outside world.

What is the rudest question you can ask a woman? "How old are you?" "What do you weigh?" "When you and your twin sister are alone with Mr. Hefner, do you have to pretend to be lesbians?" No, the worst question is "How do you juggle it all?"

"How do you juggle it all?" people constantly ask me, with an accusatory look in their eyes. "You're fucking it *all* up, aren't you?" their eyes say. My standard answer is that I have the same struggles as any working parent but with the good fortune to be working at my dream job.

The long version of the answer is more complicated.

When my daughter was about two, I was convinced that our babysitter was cutting her fingernails too short. They looked red sometimes, and she was going below the white part; it was all wrong, in my opinion. I know you're thinking that the obvious thing to do would be to point this out to the babysitter. Hear me out.

I can tell twenty comedy writers what to do; I can argue with a cabdriver about 10th Avenue versus the West Side Highway; I will happily tell a joke about Osama bin Laden or the Ku Klux Klan on live television; but I could not talk to the babysitter about the fingernail clipping. I'll bet you Margaret Thatcher would say the same thing if she were alive today.*

Here's the truth: I couldn't tell the woman who so lovingly and devotedly watches my kid every day that I didn't like how she did this one thing. I didn't want to hurt her feelings.

And here's the next layer of truth: As someone who grew up middle-class with no nannies or housekeepers of any kind, I didn't know how to handle it. I was not just a first-time mother, I was a first-time cross-cultural nanny-communicator and I was broken. Maybe that's what I should tell the roving reporter from *Showbiz Hollywood* the next time she asks me, "Is it weird for you being the boss of all these people?" "Who? These actors and teamsters and camera guys? These dummies don't scare me. Now, can you call my house and tell the babysitter I'm gonna be forty minutes late? Pweeeeze?"

But here's the deep truth: I didn't want to spend MY PRECIOUS TIME AT HOME having an awkward conversation with the babysitter. I JUST WANT TO BE

---

* Apparently Margaret Thatcher is alive and says of course she would have told the nanny directly about the problem and she thinks I am a complete chickenshit.

WITH MY KID. That's what it comes down to, really. The best days are the ones where you pass the babysitter* in the elevator, all smiles, and your apartment contains no one but your family when you walk in the door. I think my babysitter would agree. But I'm scared to ask her.

I would think of Midge's little fingers in the middle of a busy workday. I would tell myself, "Once I have the baby full-time to myself, everything will be easier." And then it hit me; that day was not coming. This "work" thing was not going away. There was no prolonged stretch of time in sight when it would just be the baby and me. And then I sobbed in my office for ten minutes. The same ten minutes that magazines urge me to use for sit-ups and triceps dips, I used for sobbing. Of course I'm not supposed to admit that there is triannual torrential sobbing in my office, because it's bad for the feminist cause. It makes it harder for women to be taken seriously in the workplace. It makes it harder for other working moms to justify their choice. But I have friends who stay home with their kids and they also have a triannual sob, so I think we should call it even. I think we should be kind to one another about it. I think we should agree to blame the children. Also, my crying three times a year doesn't distract me from my job any more than my male coworkers get distracted watching

---

* I know it's bullshit that I say "babysitter" instead of nanny. What I have is a full-time nanny, and I should be roundly punished for trying to make it seem like the teenager next door comes over one night a week. But I don't like the word "nanny." It gives me class anxiety and race anxiety. And that is why I will henceforth refer to our nanny as our Coordinator of Toddlery.

March Madness or shooting one another with Nerf guns, or (to stop generalizing) spending twenty minutes on the phone booking a doggy hotel for their pit bull before a trip to Italy with their same-sex partners.

After sobbing, I always fantasize about quitting my job. "We don't need a lot of money!" I tell myself. "We don't live extravagantly; we just live in an expensive city. If we moved to a little house in the middle of Pennsylvania we could live like kings for much less! And we'd all be together all day and we'd make cupcakes and plant a garden! And I would be taller! Yes, somehow I would be taller." My reverie is inevitably interrupted by someone who needs me to get back to work. There are almost two hundred people who work on this TV show with me. A lot of them have kids that they miss all day just like me; they keep the same terrible hours as I do; but unlike me, they are not working at their dream job. They need this job to pay their bills, and if I flaked out and quit, their jobs would disappear.

Also, there are many moments of my work that are deeply satisfying and fun. And almost as many moments of full-time motherhood that stink like Axe body spray on a brick of bleu cheese.*

So what did I do about the kid's nails? I hope you don't think I let my little one walk around with sore fingers.

---

* These moments include: cleaning poop out of a one-piece bathing suit, getting kicked in the tits by someone who doesn't want to put on her shoes, *Dora the Explorer*.

I did the logical thing, or at least what counts as logical in the fancy life I have made for myself. First thing in the morning while my daughter was on the potty I would cut her nails before I left for work. At first she didn't want to (understandably, since she was used to it hurting a little), but I convinced her by cutting the nails almost all the way left to right and then letting her have the honor of pulling the clipping the rest of the way off.* The process was preposterously slow, but we were huddled together and we told stories as we went. This is one of the weird things about motherhood. You can't predict that some of your best moments will happen around the toilet at six A.M. while you're holding a pile of fingernail clippings like a Santeria priestess.

It's three years later now, so I'd like to believe the household communication has gotten easier. For example, I can whisper to my now five-year-old kid, "Tell Jessie not to cut your nails so short. Bye!" and run away. My daughter and I can have real conversations now. I told her that I didn't like it that the mommy in the book was a witch. That it hurt my feelings. And she looked at me matter-of-factly and said, "Mommy. I can't read. I thought it was a Halloween book."

---

* By the way, I also ended up cutting them too short half the time. Apparently children just have very small fingernails. My apologies to Jessie.

The Mother's Prayer for Its Daughter

First, Lord: No tattoos. May neither the Chinese symbol for truth nor Winnie-the-Pooh holding the FSU logo stain her tender haunches.

May she be Beautiful but not Damaged, for it's the Damage that draws the creepy soccer coach's eye, not the Beauty.

When the Crystal Meth is offered,
May she remember the parents who cut her grapes in half
And stick with Beer.

Guide her, protect her
When crossing the street, stepping onto boats, swimming in the ocean, swimming in pools, walking near pools, standing on the subway platform, crossing 86th Street, stepping off of boats, using mall restrooms, getting on and off escalators, driving on country roads while arguing, leaning on large windows, walking in

262 • Tina Fey

parking lots, riding Ferris wheels, roller-coasters, log
flumes, or anything called "Hell Drop," "Tower of
Torture," or "The Death Spiral Rock 'N Zero G Roll
featuring Aerosmith," and standing on any kind of
balcony ever, anywhere, at any age.

Lead her away from Acting but not all the way to
Finance.
Something where she can make her own hours but still
feel intellectually fulfilled and get outside sometimes
And not have to wear high heels.

What would that be, Lord? Architecture? Midwifery?
Golf course design? I'm asking You, because if I knew,
I'd be doing it, Youdammit.

May she play the Drums to the fiery rhythm of her
Own Heart with the sinewy strength of her Own
Arms, so she need Not Lie With Drummers.

Grant her a Rough Patch from twelve to seventeen.
Let her draw horses and be interested in Barbies for
much too long,
For Childhood is short — a Tiger Flower blooming
Magenta for one day —
And Adulthood is long and Dry-Humping in Cars
will wait.

O Lord, break the Internet forever,
That she may be spared the misspelled invective of
her peers
And the online marketing campaign for Rape Hostel
V: Girls Just Wanna Get Stabbed.

And when she one day turns on me and calls me a
Bitch in front of Hollister,
Give me the strength, Lord, to yank her directly into a
cab in front of her friends,
For I will not have that Shit. I will not have it.

And should she choose to be a Mother one day, be my
eyes, Lord,
That I may see her, lying on a blanket on the floor at
4:50 A.M., all-at-once exhausted, bored, and in love
with the little creature whose poop is leaking up its
back.
"My mother did this for me once," she will realize as
she cleans feces off her baby's neck. "My mother did
this for me." And the delayed gratitude will wash over
her as it does each generation and she will make a Mental Note to call me. And she will forget.
But I'll know, because I peeped it with Your God eyes.

Amen

What Turning Forty
Means to Me

I need to take my pants off as soon as I get home. I didn't used to have to do that. But now I do.

What Should I Do with My Last Five Minutes?

So here we are near the end of the book, and I have a question with which I need your help. What should I do with my last five minutes? It feels like my last five minutes of being famous are timing out to be simultaneous with my last five minutes of being able to have a baby.

Science shows that fertility and movie offers drop off steeply for women after forty.

I have one top-notch baby with whom I am in love. It's a head-over-heels "first love" kind of thing, because I pay for everything and all we do is hold hands.

When she says, "I wish I had a baby sister," I am stricken with guilt and panic. When she says, *"Mommy, I need Aqua Sand,"* or "I only want to eat gum!" or "Wipe my butt!" I am less affected.

I thought that raising an only child would be the norm in Manhattan, but my daughter is the only child in her class without a sibling. Most kids have at least two. Large families have become a status symbol in New York. Four beautiful children named after kings and pieces of fruit are a way of saying "I can afford a four-bedroom apartment and $150,000 in elementary school tuition fees each year. How *you* livin'?"

Now, I'm not really one for status symbols. I went to public school. I have all my original teeth and face parts. When left to my own devices, I dress like I'm here to service your aquarium. But the kid pressure mounts for other reasons.

The woman who runs my local toy store that sells the kind of beautiful wooden educational toys that kids love (if there are absolutely no other toys around and they have never seen television) asks me, "Are you gonna have another one?"

A background actor on the set of *30 Rock* will ask, "You want more kids?" "No, no," I want to say. "Why would I want more kids when I could be here with you having an awkward conversation over a tray of old danishes?"

The ear, nose, and throat doctor I see about some stress-induced canker sores offers, unsolicited: "You should have another one. I had my children at forty-one and forty-two. It's fine." Did she not hear the part about the *stress-induced* canker sores?

My parents raised me that you never ask people about their reproductive plans. "You don't know their situation," my mom would say. I considered it such an impolite question that for years I didn't even ask myself. Thirty-five turned into forty faster than McDonald's food turns into cold nonfood.

Behind door number two, you have the movie business. Shouldn't I seize the opportunity to make more movies in the next few years? Think of the movies I could make!

- *Magazine Lady* — The story of an overworked woman looking for love ... whose less-attractive friend ...'s mean boss is played by me ... when Bebe Neuwirth turns it down.
- *The Wedding Creeper* — An overworked woman looking for love sneaks into weddings and wishes strangers well on their wedding videos, only to fall in love with a handsome videographer (Gerard Butler or a coatrack with a leather jacket on it), despite the fact that when they first met, they knocked over a wedding cake, causing an old lady (Academy Award™ winner Jane Fonda) to rap.
- Next, a strategically chosen small part in a respectable indie dramedysemble called *Disregarding Joy,* in which I play a lesbian therapist who unexpectedly cries during her partner's nephew's bris. Roger Ebert will praise my performance as "brave to grow that little mustache."
- Finally, for money, I play the villain in the live-action Moxie Girlz movie opposite a future child star who at this moment is still a tickly feeling in Billy Ray Cyrus's balls.

How could I pass up those opportunities? Do I even have the right to deprive moviegoers of those experiences?

These are the baby-versus-work life questions that keep me up at night. There's another great movie idea! *Baby Versus Work*. A hardworking baby looking for love (Kate Hudson) falls for a handsome pile of papers (Hugh Grant). I would play the ghost of a Victorian poetess who anachronistically tells Kate to "Go for it."

I debate the second-baby issue when I can't sleep. "Should I? No. I want to. I can't. I must. Of course not. I should try immediately."

I get up to go to the bathroom and study myself in the mirror. Do I look like someone who should be pregnant? I look good for forty, but I have the quaggy jawline and hollow cheeks of a mom, not a pregnant lady. It's now or never. This decision cannot be delayed.

And what's so great about work anyway? Work won't visit you when you're old. Work won't drive you to get a mammogram and take you out after for soup. It's too much pressure on my one kid to expect her to shoulder all those duties alone. Also, what if she turns on me? I am pretty hard to like. I need a backup.

And who will be my daughter's family when my husband and I are dead from stress-induced cankers? She must have a sibling. Hollywood be damned. I'll just be unemployable and labeled crazy in five years anyway.

Let me clarify. I have observed that women, at least in comedy, are labeled "crazy" after a certain age.

FEMALE WRITER: You ever work with ▮▮▮▮▮▮▮▮?
MALE AGENT: (dismissive) She's crazy now.

FEMALE WRITER: You know who I loved growing up?
██████ Mc████. What about her for this part?
MALE WRITER: I don't know. I hear she's pretty batshit.
FEMALE WRITER: I got a call today from ███████████.
MALE PRODUCER: Ugh. We had her on the show once.
She was a crazy assache. She wanted to see her lines
ahead of time. She had all these questions.

I've known older men in comedy who can barely feed and clean themselves, and they still work. The women, though, they're all "crazy."

I have a suspicion—and hear me out, 'cause this is a rough one—I have a suspicion that the definition of "crazy" in show business is a woman who keeps talking even after no one wants to fuck her anymore.

The only person I can think of that has escaped the "crazy" moniker is Betty White, which, obviously, is because people still want to have sex with her.

This is the infuriating thing that dawns on you one day: Even if you would never sleep with or even flirt with anyone to get ahead, you are being sexually adjudicated by these LA creeps. Network executives really do say things like "I don't know. I don't want to fuck anybody on this show." They really do say that stuff. That's not just lactation-stopping dialogue on *Entourage*.

(To any exec who has ever said that about me, I would hope you would at least have the intelligence and self-awareness to know that the feeling is extremely mutual.)

It seems to me that the fastest remedy for this "Women

Are Crazy" situation is for more women to become producers and hire diverse women of various ages. That is why I feel obligated to stay in the business and try hard to get to a place where I can create opportunities for others, and that's why I can't possibly take time off for a second baby, unless I *do,* in which case that is nobody's business and I'll never regret it for a moment unless it ruins my life.

And now it's four o'clock in the morning.

To hell with everybody! Maybe I'll just wait until I'm fifty and give birth to a ball of fingers! "Merry Christmas from Tina, Jeff, Alice, and Ball of Fingers," the card will say. ("Happy Holidays" on the ones I send to my agents.)

I try to think about anything else so I can fall back to sleep. I used to cling to the fact that my mom had me unexpectedly at forty, only to realize a couple years ago that I had the math wrong and she was thirty-nine. A world of difference, in my insomniac opinion.

My mom was conceived in the US, born in Greece, and brought back here as an infant. Because of this, she never gets jury duty.

She grew up speaking both languages, and when I was in elementary school she volunteered to be a classroom aide because a lot of the Greeks in our neighborhood were "right off the boat," as she would say, and needed a translator. My mother knew the language and the culture. Sometimes the teachers would ask her to translate bad news. "Please tell Mrs. Fondulas that her son is very disruptive." And my mom would nod and say in Greek,

"George is a lovely boy." Because she knew if she really translated that, the kid would get a beating and the mother would hate her forever out of embarrassment.

Little kids' birthdays in my neighborhood were simple affairs. Hot dogs, Hawaiian Punch, pin the tail on the donkey, followed by cake and light vomiting. (Wieners, punch, and spinning into barfing would later be referred to as "the Paris Hilton.")

I would always complain to my mother after the Greek kids' parties because they served Italian rum cake.

Covered in slivered almonds and soaked in booze, Italian rum cake is everything kids hate about everything. No one even ate it. It just got thrown away.

Cake Time is supposed to be the climax of a birthday, but instead it was a crushing disappointment for all. I imagine it's like being at a bachelor party only to find that the stripper has overdosed in the bathroom.

After a couple years of this nonsense my mom explained to me that the reason the "Greeky Greeks," as she called them, got the Italian rum cakes was because they were the most expensive item in the bakery. They wanted the adults at the party to know they could afford it. Anyway, is that what I'm trying to do with this second-baby nonsense? Am I just chasing it because it's the hardest thing for me to get and I want to prove I can do it?

Do I want another baby? Or do I just want to turn back time and have my daughter be a baby again?

Some of you must be thinking, "Well, what does your husband want? He's a part of this decision, too, you know!" He wants me to stop agonizing, but neither of us knows whether that means go for it or move on.

Why not do both, like everybody else in the history of earth? Because, as I think we have established in this book, things most people do naturally are often inexplicably difficult for me. Secondly, the math is impossible. No matter how you add up the months, it means derailing the TV show where two hundred people depend on me for their income, and I take that stuff seriously. Like everyone from Tom Shales to Jeff Zucker, I thought *30 Rock* would be cancelled by now.

I have a great gynecologist who is as gifted at listening as she is at rectal exams. I went for my annual checkup and, tired of carrying this anxiety around, burst into tears the moment she said hello. I laid it all out for her, and the main thing I took away from our conversation was the kind of simple observation that only an impartial third party can provide. "Either way, everything will be fine," she smiled, and for a little while I was pulled out of my anxious, stunted brain cloud.

One time my mom babysat a set of the Italian Rum Cake Kids while their parents went to a wedding reception. This was the first time this nice couple had gone out alone since their children were born. Their parents dropped them off after the ceremony. Little Christo and Maria were still all dressed up. Christo wore a tiny black suit and a white shirt. Maria wore a red velvet dress and cried in the playpen from the moment her parents left until the moment they returned. My mom tried everything to console her, food... The end.

After a couple hours of this, seven-year-old Christo was beside himself. He had never been babysat before. How long was this fuckery going to go on? His sister was hysterical. He paced around our living room, now in his shirtsleeves and black pants. Pulling his golden curls nervously, he looked like the night manager of a miniature diner who had just had a party of six dine and dash. He ranted to his baby sister in Greek, "Πως καταντήσαμε, βρε Μαρία!" This sent my mother running into the dining room laughing hysterically. I chased her. What? What did he say? Roughly translated it was "Oh! My Maria! What is to become of us?"

His overdramatic ridiculousness tickled my mom in such a specific way that she was doubled over in the dining room, hoping the kids wouldn't see that she was laughing so hard at them she peed a little. A phenomenon I now understand on all levels.

They were going to be fine, but they couldn't possibly believe it.

That must have been what I looked like to my doctor friend. That must be what I look like to anyone with a real problem—active-duty soldier, homeless person, Chilean miner, etc. A little tiny person with nothing to worry about running in circles, worried out of her mind.

Either way, everything will be fine. But if you have an opinion, please feel free to offer it to me through the gap in the door of a public restroom. Everyone else does.

Acknowledgments

I would like to gratefully thank: Kay Cannon, Richard Dean, Eric Gurian, John Riggi, and Tracey Wigfield for their eyes and ears. Dave Miner for making me do this. Reagan Arthur for teaching me how to do this. Katie Miervaldis for her dedicated service and Latvian demeanor. Tom Ceraulo for his mad computer skills. Michael Donaghy for two years of Sundays.

Jeff and Alice Richmond for their constant loving encouragement and their constant loving interruption, respectively.

Thank you to Lorne Michaels, Marc Graboff, and NBC for allowing us to reprint material.

About the Author

Tina Fey lives in Denver with her ferret, Jacoby.

Reading Group Guide

Bossypants

by

Tina Fey

Tina Fey answers her fans' questions from Twitter

@Dantea21: What was the writing process for Bossypants *like compared to your scripted comedies?*

Writing a book is a solitary experience. I would hide from my own family in a tiny room next to our washer/dryer and type. To keep the writing from being too stiff, I tried to imagine I was having a conversation with a friend. Writing for television is more of a group process. You have a bunch of conversations with a room full of friends and then pretend you came up with them alone by your washer/dryer.

When the book is complete, you are able to buy a better washer/dryer.

@candygreen: Many girls consider you an idol due to your high awesomeness quotient. Who gave you inspiration growing up?

Carol Burnett, Dorothy Hamill, Miss Piggy, Jan Hooks, Betsy Ross, Amanda Whurlitzer.

@candygreen: Also—can we get Korean manicures together, please?

@candygreen: Yes, meet me at the cleanish one on 75th and Lex in an hour.

@candygreen: I'm here. Where are you?

@candygreen: Virgin Orchid or Adore-a-Ball? Also, what color should I get?

@candygreen: Are you coming?

@candygreen: I'm trying to save the pedicure seat next to mine, but this stuck-up B with her damn dog is giving me the stink eye.

@candygreen: Actually, maybe she's blind. Disregard.

@candygreen: Will I regret Turquoise and Caicos? Where are u?!

@candygreen: These answers are going out on Twitter, right? P.S.: Total T&C regret.

@candygreen: Okay, I checked. Apparently these answers are only being printed in a book several months after you submit them.

@candygreen: I'll still just wait here for you.

@candygreen: Where r u?

@Ellielondon: Have you ever not been able to keep a straight face on set during SNL?

I don't think I've ever "broken" on *SNL*. Mostly because if someone's being really funny, you don't want to mess up their thing by laughing. Of course on Weekend Update, the anchors kind of have permission to laugh at the jokes and features if we want to, so we have it much easier than the people sitting next to Debbie Downer.

@ColleenPGreen: Tina Fey, what was the moment you knew you wanted to get into comedy?

When I lost the last spot on the 1992 U.S. Olympic basketball team to Clyde Drexler.

@Goodgodgaelle: Would you like to rewrite the chapter about the asking of a second child? Or add something, now that you have another one?

I don't think I will rewrite that chapter because it describes a very specific period of panic in my life that other people may recognize in themselves. Also, nobody made Rupert Holmes rewrite "The Piña Colada Song" after it turned out his personal ad was answered by his own wife at the end. So...

@kaitmarch: Tina, because all of humankind has the sandwich in common: Jimmy John's, Wawa hoagies, or cheesesteaks?

I would say you got the order exactly right. Jimmy John's is the best. I recommend the Vegetarian. Amy Poehler prefers a place called Potbelly. It's one of the few things we strongly disagree about. The other is the movie *Love Actually*. I won't say which side we each take on that. Anyway, back to sandwiches. The Wawa Italian hoagie is a very close second—oil and vinegar, no mayonnaise, of course. Thirdliciously, a cheesesteak with provolone cheese from Jim's Steaks on South Street in Philadelphia.

@Flowwiththeflo: Tina, where'd you get your colonial-lady Halloween costume?! I may or may not want one…

My colonial-lady costume was mostly a hand-me-down burlap maxi-skirt from my cousin, but I was able to supplement it at the time with items like mobcaps and long woolen socks from area museum stores and Revolutionary War reenactment sites. (Remember, I had an advantage growing up in the *real* "real America," between Philadelphia and Valley Forge, Pennsylvania.) Tricorn hats and replica fifes were readily available in the summer of '76. I think your best bet these days would be to troll the vendors around the perimeter of a Tea Party rally. But shop carefully; a lot of those booths are just fronts for illegal OxyContin.

@MarinaMularz: Tina, what's the best way to waste time at the DMV?

Every twenty minutes go to the back of the line again.

@TinaFey30: Tina, do you think many women or teenagers from all the world can feel identified with you?? Argentina loves you, please answer! ♥

I am flattered to think that other women around the world might identify with me. But honestly, I'm just like everyone else. I put my pants on one leg. I drink air and breathe water, like anyone. I sleep in my bra and slowly eat the phonebook over several months.

I am Argentina. I always will be.

@PinkyTurtles: If you were stuck watching the same movie for the rest of your life, what would it be?

Annie Hall or the original *Charlie and the Chocolate Factory*.

@DKMommy: My roommate picks her nose. What should I do? Sincerely, Worried About Nosebleed

@DKMommy, there is an old improv saying: "Do it now. Do it too. Do it again." So maybe when your roommate is picking her nose, stand very close to her and pick your nose, too. (A good improviser would then "heighten" this action by picking the other side of your roommate's nose for her.) This will either startle her into realizing how disgusting she's being, or you will have found something you enjoy doing together. Either way it's what "scientists" and "people on the *Today* show" refer to as a "win, win."

@NotStephanie: Most awkward moment?

Getting my period for the first time while wearing white terry cloth shorts in front of all the members of New Kids On The Block at the exact moment I won the Scripps Howard National Spelling Bee. Luckily, I'm pretty sure this was just a dream.

@NotStephanie: Do you prefer filming for TV or movies?

I like the immediacy of TV, especially live TV, where you can make up something on a Tuesday and people are seeing it by Saturday. Movies are exciting, too, though, because when you're on a movie screen your face and your check are much larger.

Questions and topics for discussion

1) What do you think it means to be a Bossypants? Do you know anyone personally that you would describe as a Bossypants and did the society you live in ever try to drown her?

2) The lessons Tina has learned from her work as a writer, a boss, a performer, and a producer are lessons that can be carried across a wide array of disciplines. (For instance, from her instructions about improv: Always speak in statements.) Which moments resonated the most for you?

3) In Chapter 4, Tina realizes that she has been guilty of holding her gay friends to a double standard — enjoying their company but still expecting them to stay in a "half-closet." Have you ever had a moment like this? In a related question, do you think young pop stars today experience too much pressure to pretend to be a lesbian with Madonna?

4) While working at the YMCA in Chicago, Tina experienced some personal low points. But it also propelled her into pursuing her improv career. Have you ever experienced a similarly transformative period? During your transformation, did you ever spin around and pretend to be Wonder Woman?

5) What are some of your favorite *SNL* sketches or *30 Rock* episodes? Should we just act them out?

6) Which other celebrities, besides Kim Kardashian, do you think may have been engineered by Russian scientists to sabotage our athletes?

7) Are there more specifics you would add to "The Mother's Prayer for Its Daughter"?

8) Tina writes a love letter to Amy Poehler. Do you have friends who inspire you in the same way that Amy inspires Tina?

   ACTIVITY: Write a love letter to Amy Poehler and mail it to her home address (p. 291).

Available from Hachette Digital

BOSSYPANTS

Unabridged audiobook, read by Tina Fey –
available on CD or download

Enhanced ebook edition

Includes Special, Never-Before-Solicited Opinions on
Breastfeeding, Princesses, Photoshop, the Electoral
Process, and Italian Rum Cake! This Enhanced eBook
experience also includes special audio clips from Tina Fey,
speculation on what an eBook really is, a bonus section of
new-to-you photos, interpretive drawings, and a chapter
read by the author!

Available wherever ebooks are sold.